THE BIG NO

Center for 21st Century Studies

Kennan Ferguson, Series Editor

THE BIG NO

Kennan Ferguson, Editor

Center for 21st Century Studies

University of Minnesota Press
Minneapolis
London

Published by the University of Minnesota Press
111 Third Avenue South, Suite 290
Minneapolis, MN 55401–2520
http://www.upress.umn.edu

ISBN 978-1-5179-0928-4 (hc)
ISBN 978-1-5179-0929-1 (pb)

A Cataloging-in-Publication record for this book is available from the Library of Congress.

Printed in the United States of America on acid-free paper

UMP BmB 2021

Contents

Acknowledgments

During the last weekend of April 2017, the Center for 21st Century Studies (C21) at the University of Wisconsin–Milwaukee (UWM) held the conference "The Big No," where early versions of many of these essays were presented. The conference depended on the work and resourcefulness of many people. First and foremost were the organizing committee, particularly Alison Sperling (deputy director, 2015–16) and Kalling Heck (deputy director, 2016–17). John Blum, the center's associate director, proved invaluable in the coordination of speakers and essays. Both Cami Thomas and Leila Saboori assisted in writing, publicizing, and organizing speakers and volunteers.

Such events are impossible without considerable financial support from institutions and organizations. At UWM, thanks to Johannes Britz, provost and vice chancellor for academic affairs; the College of Letters and Science (Jasmine Alinder, interim dean of humanities, and Dave Clark, interim dean); Marija Gajdardziska-Josifovska, dean of the Graduate School; and Mark Harris, interim vice provost for research. Additional funding was provided by the William F. Vilas Trust, which supports faculty, students, and arts at UW–Madison and UWM.

The editing, indexing, and production of this book depended centrally on Maureen Ryan, current deputy director of the center. Maureen's tireless work with authors, publishers, and directors of C21 has been astonishing to behold. Thanks also to Zenyse Miller, Danielle Kasprzak, and Doug Armato at the University of Minnesota Press. Finally, my gratitude to this book's contributors, who were willing to undergo challenges from me, from one another, from reviewers, and from the world at large to engage problems and questions with an undeniably negative charge.

Introduction

No Politics

Kennan Ferguson

What are the politics of no? Naysaying has considerable power, but scholars have insufficiently theorized its potential. The presumption that political action is always positive—that it must lead to something programmatic and organized—obscures the potentials of outright refusal for many kinds of thinking and action. No is pregnant with possibilities, promises, and dangers. Above all, it is political.

In cultures of capitalist consumption, no has the power to defend and upend assumptions of propriety and permanence. From Thoreau to Gandhi to Marcuse, the will to nothing has provided a source of individual and collective creation.[1] Refusals dramatically reshape politics, nationhood, sovereignty, and land. Each historical emergence of no surprises and confounds observers, while bringing new convergences to political organizations. Twice over the past seventy-five years, the Greeks have famously declared their own version of no, "OXI"; Brexiteers voted against remaining in the European Union; French Yellow Vests Protests; Native Americans (and their allies) from across the North American continent came together against the Dakota Access Pipeline in a collective refusal. Even much of Donald Trump's support in the 2016 election seemed to arise more from a desire to throw out the old system than from an attraction to the candidate himself. No promises, seduces, and appeals in its pure negativity.

The concept of no may decline alternatives; it may have nothing "productive" about it. The naysayer, the Bartleby, the refusenik, the denier, the antagonist, the disavower, the invalidator: such people, we generally presume, are best avoided. "No" and "the negative" are practically synonymous; no blocks, refuses, and declines rather than celebrating, consoling, or creating.

We, too, often expend excessive time and energy trying to achieve a yes. The promise of yes is the demand of adulthood, of "constructive engagement," of putting the solution first and the sense of grievance and outrage second. This promise underpins the familiar demands that one cannot criticize without an alternative, that people who complain or refuse or block must build an entirely different world before that complaint or refusal or blocking can be considered valid, that every unhappy person proves responsible for his or her own unhappiness.

Yes is a modality of power. It demands productivity and contemporaneity, insisting on the development of full-blown alternatives, while declaiming responsibility for extant conditions. Yes frames issues in two ways, presuming that the extant world has already been fully imagined and completed, while also necessitating, requiring an involvement with that reality. It implicitly legitimizes the contemporary world. Aiming for yes means compromising in advance. It is to allow that to get somewhere, you must start where you are. Yes is agreeable; yes is conciliatory; yes is complicit.

Contrary to these assumptions, what might it mean to celebrate the potential and the power of no? For no stands against consensus, against assumption, against presumption, against the easy passage. No emerges early and maintains its appeal and power—it is available to one and all. No may be instinctual, or it may be carefully constructed, but in either case, it disturbs order and propriety, forcing power to act nakedly and bringing to the forefront the implicit and accepted.

Theoretical attention to negativity has developed in recent years from a variety of sources. Queer theory has been central to this emergence, at least in the United States. In the face of the social demand of procreative sexuality—the presumption that human pleasure must perpetuate the continuation of the species—a wide range of critical sexuality scholars have staged a denial of service. Bodies themselves create and experience pleasure; desire exceeds generation. To reject the link of sex and generation, they showed, was to recapture the power of physicality, desire, and the present.

In some cases, this entailed a rejection of the entire social sphere. Following Eve Kosofsky Sedgwick's insight that men's desire for one another makes up social order, both by denying their own erotics and through excluding women, queer theorists demanded an end to extant social relations.[2] In other cases, these intuitions demanded a rejection of futurity itself, most famously in Lee Edelman's *No Future,* but also in the earlier work of Guy Hocquenghem or the alternative counterpublics of Michael Warner.[3] More recently, theorists such as Jack Halberstam, David Eng, and José Muñoz have attempted to recuperate the social without rejecting the power of no.[4]

As these debates show, not all nos are equivalent; they are neither exchangeable with one another in their capacities nor active in the same ways. No is illiquid, nonfungible. One way to start thinking about this volume is by classifying a few different kinds of no, a set of negativities easily but inappropriately confused. This is not a claim that the following typology is complete (no constantly surprises), but it may serve as a useful mapping of some of the gravitational centers in the galaxy of nos that politics provides.

The first sort of no—the one most commonly associated with its utterance—is the no of resistance. This is the no of both the two-year-old and the subversive. It says, simply, that the current situation does not work. Such a naysayer may recognize the compulsory power of the system she or he confronts but stand against it nonetheless. A resistor says no to reject the assumptions that we must all get to a yes, to deny that cooperation with a system (be it evil, inhumane, or just plain enervating) remains always and forever necessary. The space of resistances is the no of the subversive and the saboteur, those who find that the best way to use their wooden shoe is to throw it in the machine. One declines to work, to grieve, to love, to support, to acquiesce, to comply, to participate. This constitutes the negativity of "enough, already." It is immediately accessible, easy, even: ever present in a country song or a daydream. It is far too often obscured by the ideologies of necessity, of adulthood, of responsibility. The no of resistance is best prefaced or followed by obscenity.

This first no is easily recognized as political. When an anthropologist identifies the way a village resists the state, or a literary critic notes how a mode of writing undermines absolute authorship, or a journalist describes how adolescents upset their parents, each identifies a no that transforms the normal operations of power. Such naysaying does not overthrow extant power but rather attempts to interrupt it, depriving it of its totality.

At its most extreme, this is the no of revolution, of the complete (or at least as far as the imagination can reach) overthrow of the existing social order. But as this no becomes embedded in political action, it turns to questions of efficacious naysaying: how best to stop being what others want? Thus the Marx who calls for the overthrow of capitalism cannot be separated from the Marx who entreats workers to join together in union and other modes of solidarity; the Fanon who finds racial self-recognition and social unity the antidote to colonial oppression connects closely to the Fanon who replicates the European nation-state as the requisite form of revolutionary activity.

Joshua Clover finds in both of these thinkers a set of overlapping concerns that bring out the potential of collective action in the contemporary economic system. Who holds the ultimate ability to enact the revolutionary no? For Marx, only and specifically the worker, men stripped of historical significance by capitalism who ultimately come to see their identity as communally powerful. For Fanon, a century later, the urbanized *lumpen*, the marginalized men and women of the colonial city. What do these incipient collectivities have in common? A particular combination: their exclusion from power, conjoined to their economic and political indispensability. They are thus promised inclusion (but only at the cost of disappearance) and welcome (but only against the reality of discrimination and disenfranchisement). The relationship between these two, what Clover terms "absorption" and "coloniality," forces different groups of people to the indefinite perimeters. Thus the structural similarities of urban Detroit, suburban Paris, and occupied lands everywhere.

Such societal disempowerment also leads to individual forms of naysaying. Take, for example, the category of the antisocial.

What kind of person deserves such an appellation? One who not only rejects the stultified, accepted modes of behavior common to polite society but also actively strives against the society as a whole. To withdraw or ignore social norms does not suffice: the result becomes mere loneliness or desolation. The truly antisocial actor destroys the expectations of those around him, not to (pleasurably) shock but to undermine and threaten.

Theodore Martin finds various representations of this form in the novel. This particular genre embodies a certain method of withdrawal, for example, in the privacy of reading, while also developing a celebration of particular modes of antisocialism. The critical interrogation of "society" as a collective concept—of the idea that we owe our own totality to one another—begins to give way in the twentieth century to a more independent, supporting, autonomously authorizing self. This sort of person could be seen as the liberal individual beloved of capitalist consumption; conversely, such a person is a sociopath. Novelists such as Patricia Highsmith, Jim Thompson, and Richard Wright manage, in their presentation of antisocial characters, to destabilize the opposition between the purported pathology of social iconoclasts and social conformists.

This resistant no operates in multiple places and is practiced by many people. The contemporary condition—the "way things are"—makes very few people happy and thus drives many toward impedance: they undercut their superiors, they slack off, they fidget, they redirect. Throwing sand in the gears feels good. Slowing down the machine proves pleasing, watching it slow and stall. Those in positions of domination, servility, and obeisance easily grasp the general appeal of no. The no of resistance provides its own rewards.

A second form of no might be termed the no of forking paths. This no imagines a completionist auxiliary. Rather than accepting the given, this no puts in its place a whole set of alternative possibilities and effects. Rather than life, for example, it demands liberty, or the pursuit of happiness. Rejecting one or more precondition, such a no replaces it with another condition and traces the results and implications of this alterity. This is the no of science fiction, counterfactual history, and non-philosophy.[5]

The conception of non-Euclidean geometry may best metaphorize this second no, where one or more of the commonly accepted premises of geometry are denied. For example, what happens when one replaces the axiom that parallel lines never meet, assuming instead that they meet at infinity? One then can work through the math of manifolds and other nonhomeomorphic figures.[6] The partiality of such a no can initially seem minimal or even irrelevant (what's one postulate among friends?), but its implications grow and expand as the consequences build on one another. The stream of the new no flows alongside the original riverbed, often leaving it alone; in time it may become its own powerful force. At times the novel may even outweigh the source. Nonstandards can fractally become standards, and vice versa, of course, and can themselves generate their own alternatives. Such a no is unlimitedly generative, creating from its rejection a new mathematics and a new universe of understanding.

This no is more than mathematical. It can be theological: against monotheism, it might insist on polytheism, or animism, or materialism. It can be biological: Darwin's positing humans as merely one sort of animal among many others rather than a wholly separate kind of being. It can be technological: a rejection of developing artificial intelligence through programming and its replacement with machine learning. It can be conceptual: Freud arguing that consciousness cannot apprehend itself. Whether a new science, technique, or idea, each starts with a profound rejection, developing an alternative from that active rejection. In each case, an entirely new set of results and conclusions emerges from the processes of negativity.

Philosophy itself emerges from the naysaying of experience—as a system of thought, it makes claims to a reality *more real* than what humans see, feel, and sense. Though this claim is the Platonic precondition to philosophical thought, contemporary philosophy has returned to the potentiality of rejecting Plato's hierarchical dualism. What if the mind, for example, and consequently thought itself, operates as a bodily and material reality? What, in other words, if philosophy cannot depend on its own presumptions and fails to justify itself?

The next essays in this volume evoke this second kind of no through the work of François Laruelle, whose explorations of what he previously termed "non-philosophy" attempt to open up alternative ways of thinking and being. The formalized kind of thinking that has operated under the name of "philosophy" depends on a number of preconditions: the presumption that philosophy operates as a master discourse of understanding, that reality is only that which can be logically and properly thought, that the conceptual portioning of different kinds of things from one another (e.g., art, knowledge, truth) reflects a kind of actual difference.[7] The rejection of any of these presuppositions undercuts philosophy's self-authorization.

François Laruelle's essay describes how the distance between the work of Gilles Deleuze and Jacques Derrida stages a relationship between the negative and the affirmative. Both thinkers attempt to negotiate the claims of negativity to achieve an overcoming of the patterns of thought, in one case with the suspension of unity and in the other with *différance*. But both Deleuze and Derrida fall under the spell of the promise of language embedded in such overcoming—the idea that philosophy itself can transcend its own limitations, that its own differences are transformative rather than additive. In contrast, Laruelle argues, philosophy must reject its very presumptive separation from the immanence of the world. The streams of Greek thought, along which both Deleuze and Derrida continue to pilot, reinforce an absolutism of abstraction and causality; Laruelle, in contrast, follows similar contours to immanent and emergent realities.

Katerina Kolozova develops another form of the no that builds alternatives. Her no denies the presumption that philosophy can entirely and appropriately engage concrete materiality. Like Marx, Saussure, and Laruelle, Kolozova notes the inability of philosophical logic to account for its own predilection toward signification. The real—a critically important term for Kolozova—can never be reduced to thought, no matter the insistence of the human-centric nature of thinking. Instead, the real and thought operate coterminously, each in a separate realm of legitimation, discovery, and continuity. The abstractions foisted on the real, including those of philosophy, form the preconditions of its transformation into a manipulable "clone." This process, Kolozova notes, allows for capitalism, alienation, and technological automata.

Each of these approaches to the second no—the no of the forking path—denies a central assumption in philosophical history. Rejecting the accretions that have built up around these assumptions allows for new creations and substitute conceptual realities. Much as speculative fiction presumes certain developments to build future worlds, these branches of philosophical naysaying allow alternative paths of thinking, truth, and relationality. The preeminent difference, however, is that such a world may already be with us.

The third sort of no is the no of absolute refusal, of confrontational negation, of abolition. This no not only avoids participation; it also points to the world that its own utterance opens up. This is the refusal of the conscientious objection, the Native sovereignty, and the literary dissident. In some ways, this draws from the first two forms of no, in that it rejects the status quo and looks elsewhere. But it differs from them by its very existence standing against the thing it opposes. To archaism, such a naysayer posits anarchism—to consensus, dissensus; to order, laughter.

The archetypal sentence for this third approach begins "But, no . . ." It rejects the very assumptions embedded in the request or provocation; it looks elsewhere. William Apess, the mid-nineteenth-century Pequot legal theorist, named this "Indian nullification." Laws that err, that oppress, that delegitimize entire peoples, are illegitimate. When the entire system of governance is wrong, the intentions of government agents do not matter. Indians like the Apess's Mashpee, therefore, not only have no obligation to follow laws but the laws also have no legitimate claim upon them. Even if the laws serve Natives (though, of course, they do not), they are imposed from a foreign peoples; the only proper response is what Audra Simpson calls "refusal."[8]

The refusing no breaks up the presumptions of unity, of communal experience, and of collective purpose. This no does not accept that "we are all in this together," insisting instead that historical, structural, or economic logics preclude certain kinds of people from flourishing in the current political space. Indigenous peoples may note that insurmountable barriers arise from settler-colonialism, where the history of stolen land cannot be overcome. Those nations whose lands have been colonized may point to today's global wealth gap as a direct consequence of this history, one which the world's wealthier nations will never repair. The descendants of enslaved people may underscore the theft, murder, and dismemberment of Black labor and bodies that liberal individualism not only fails to recompense but that continues in new forms in various racist societies.

To any of these perspectives, the demand for something such as reconciliation (proposed as the only possible approach to peace) seems laughable. The antireconciler thus stands against the presumption that all can and will be forgiven and overcome. Reconciliation depends on subsumption, a final synthesis of the thesis and antithesis. Thus denying reconciliation rejects the legitimacy of this synthetic absorption. Nonreconciliation stands not as a problem but as a goal—reconciliation presumes that we can ultimately "get over it." A world of antireconciliation and nonreciprocality does not reject action, politics, or meaning but rather insists on the power of co-incidence, those incidents obscured by the processes of resolution and compromise.[9] What if reconciliation obscures justice, or history, or truth? Why should it prevail? To the demand for "truth and reconciliation" the third no scoffs: these two concepts will always undermine one another, because reconciliation always demands and depends on untruths.

Occasionally this third form of no comes from a place of impossibility. The philosopher Calvin L. Warren notes that the existence of "the Negro" proves permanently foreclosed from the possibility of Being (in the Heideggerian sense): blackness founds metaphysics precisely as its outside, its irredeemable other.[10] This is not a chosen no but the no of fundamental antimony. Frank B. Wilderson III calls this no the "absence of reciprocity, utility, and contingency." Entering via autobiography, Wilderson notes the psychic cathexis that follows Black bodies. Other losses of the world—Wilderson starts with the example of the Palestinian *Nakba* and subsequent dislocation and dispossession—terrible as they are, are losses along the register of meaning. Life, land, labor: to steal these through violence constitutes the worst of politics. But this is still politics in its full relationality. The reality facing Black life, Wilderson shows through an explication of his poem "Law Abiding," denies even the violence of politics, replacing it with a violence that itself is the subject of politics. Black life, Black bodies, Black suffering: those are mere objects, stripped of the potentials of recognition or relationality.

Wilderson's no, then, refuses the trap of the promise of analogy. Anticipating a future of racial equivalence means ignoring the structural violence built into the creation and continuation of the United States. Assuming that idealism, dreams, law, or logic can combat this intrinsic violence misses the role such violence plays as fundamental, legally foundational, and prelogical. Anti-Blackness was not instaurated against some sort of promised equality but was built into the operations of power and politics.

The refusals and nonrecognitions of this no surprisingly echo the concerns of the earlier negativities. The conceptual overlaps of the no of (what has become known as) Afro-pessimism and the no of non-philosophy interest Andrew Culp. He identifies three major locations of reverberation between them: withdrawal, blackness as ontological death, and the stance of uchromia. Withdrawal, in both its secessionist and refusal forms, notes the entrapment inherent to the presumptions of participation; rather than operate as part of the ensnaring project (whether mainstream philosophy or racial reconciliation), the theoretical project builds toward nonparticipation. Blackness qua death, the second area of overlap, arises from the first. As a multitude of social critics have argued, following Orlando Patterson, Black life often counts for nothing, instead marking the absence of humanity.[11] Even the violent obliteration of Black bodies leaves little trace in the social architecture of racialized memory. The third, in which both Afro-pessimism and non-philosophy address the politics of color, leads to a reconsideration of the no of opposition. Both philosophies assert blackness as neither the reverse of whiteness nor a fully realized color itself but rather as lack, as totalized opacity. All three of these reverberations, Culp notes, result in a politics of insufficiency, a rejection of forward-looking resolutionary agreement, instead calling for radical dissent and antipathetic activism.

That "Indian nullification" has any conducive relationship with

Afro-pessimism may seem surprising. The latter (Wilderson perhaps most emphatically) often overtly compares Black experience with the rights and legitimacies of Natives in the context of U.S. history, as he does in this volume, to argue that Black people are denied the connections to history and land available to Natives. Since Afro-pessimism differentiates itself from Native claims, how can its no be akin to Indian nullification and refusal? If these varieties of refusal are all seen as related—if they are all varieties of resistance to power—such a connection is nonsensical. But the radical nature of this third no does not depend on relationality. Different kinds of absolute refusal are absolute in themselves. Refusal totalizes.

So what to make of this volume's contributors' relationship to the power of no? This typology of three nos serves merely as an introduction—each reader is encouraged to question and even scorn it. In fact, the next pages overflow with such rejections: of hierarchies, of orders, of self-possession. One kind of no may undercut and oppose another. But they are all very big nos: uncompromising, unreconciling, unbending. They all say no—against one another, and together.

One final inquiry: what makes a no into a big no? So far the power of the negative has been more important than its scale. What is it that differentiates the quotidian no, the merely stubborn no, the somewhat-recalcitrant no, from the big nos described earlier? It may be impossible to reach a clear and definitive answer, of course: the no of an outraged toddler may be huge to him or her, while simply a considerable annoyance to the parent, and only a tiny statistical point to the quantitative child psychologist. But clues remain. Each big no entails not just confrontation or contrariness but the impossibility of concession or conciliation. The bigness has less to do with the substance of the conflict, but with the reality of the opposition. Such a no will not go along, participate grudgingly, subsume itself. Instead, it will stand against power, against argument, against settlement. A desultory no can never be big; a big no will never reach only halfway.

The eruptive force of the big no transforms the argumentative landscape in every case. Whether a nation-state or a conscientious individual, the interruptive immediacy of naysaying can occur at surprising and inconvenient moments. The contexts of no involve political, economic, even physical risks, making naysaying an often difficult and complex act. No can be a language of protest and overcoming. Its power operates across lines of disciplines and ideology, across modes of writing and the refusal to write. Negation can resist or avoid authority or can identify and highlight forces that insist on forms of complicity and agreement. The lines between different forms—the conservative no, the creative no, the no of the striker or dissident—obliterate the clarity of lines of ideology or identity.

Notes

1. Henry David Thoreau, "Civil Disobedience," in *The Variorum Civil Disobedience*, 31–58 (New York: Twayne Publishers, 1967); Mohandas Karamchand Gandhi, *Gandhi, an Autobiography: The Story of My Experiments with Truth* (Boston: Beacon Press, 1957); Herbert Marcuse, *An Essay on Liberation* (Boston: Beacon Press, 1969).
2. Eve Kosofsky Sedgwick, *Between Men: English Literature and Male Homosocial Desire* (New York: Columbia University Press, 1985); Leo Bersani, *Homos* (Cambridge, Mass.: Harvard University Press, 1995); Lisa Duggan, "Queering the State," *Social Text*, no. 39 (Summer 1994): 1–14.
3. Lee Edelman, *No Future: Queer Theory and the Death Drive* (Durham, N.C.: Duke University Press, 2004); Guy Hocquenghem, *Homosexual Desire*, trans. Daniella Dangoor (Durham, N.C.: Duke University Press, 1993); Michael Warner, *Publics and Counterpublics* (Cambridge: Zone Books, 2002).
4. Judith Halberstam, *The Queer Art of Failure* (Durham, N.C.: Duke University Press, 2010); David L. Eng, *The Feeling of Kinship: Queer Liberalism and the Racialization of Intimacy* (Durham, N.C.: Duke University Press, 2010); José Esteban Muñoz, *Cruising Utopia: The Then and There of Queer Futurity* (New York: New York University Press, 2009).
5. See, e.g., François Laruelle, *Principles of Non-philosophy*, trans. Anthony Paul Smith (London: Bloomsbury Academic, 2013).
6. Using Lobachevsky–Bolyai–Gauss geometry. Using another rejection of the Euclidean parallel postulate, elliptic (or Riemannian) geometry gives a different set of possibilities.
7. See François Laruelle, "A Summary of Non-philosophy," *Pli* 8

(1999): 138–48; Alexander R. Galloway, *Laruelle: Against the Digital* (Minneapolis: University of Minnesota Press, 2014).

8. William Apess, *Indian Nullification of the Unconstitutional Laws of Massachusetts, Relative to the Marshpee Tribe; or, The Pretended Riot Explained* (Boston: Press of Jonathan Howe, 1835).
9. Afro-pessimism, for example, rejects the very idea of liberation and racial equality, noting that the United States (among other nations) was founded on the oppression of Africans and those of African descent. Racism, in other words, can never be separated from the makeup and practices of the state. Frank B. Wilderson, *Red, White, and Black: Cinema and the Structure of U.S. Antagonisms* (Durham, N.C.: Duke University Press, 2010); Jared Sexton, *Amalgamation Schemes: Antiblackness and the Critique of Multiracialism* (Minneapolis: University of Minnesota Press, 2008).
10. Calvin L. Warren, *Ontological Terror: Blackness, Nihilism, and Emancipation* (Durham, N.C.: Duke University Press, 2018), 35.
11. Orlando Patterson, *Slavery and Social Death: A Comparative Study* (Cambridge, Mass.: Harvard University Press, 1982).

1

Absorption and Coloniality

Joshua Clover

Revolution is history's Big No.[1] Who, within history's logic, might emerge to contradict that history's affirmative character? As I, like Ovid before me, am interested in nothing but transformation, I am particularly compelled by how the emergences and affordances of revolutionary actors might change over time rather than having any ontological consistency—antagonisms no matter how essential can only be understood, can only find their significance and become self-coherent, insofar as we can discern the history-making movement that gives them form and substance. I want to trace out this history-making movement as it arrives in our here and now. Inevitably we will have to start somewhere else. In fact, we will have to start with France, which is to say, against France.

Thus it should really be *Le Big Non*. We begin not with one *non* but with two, both from the movies, both from the 1960s, both involving wars against France. One from the metropole, one from the colony. The first is from a documentary made in the working-class outskirts of Paris, its title often translated as *Return to Work at the Wonder Factory*. It reaches back to the French origins of cinema, 1895's *Workers Leaving the Lumière Factory*. It is fair to say that the thematic of workers and factories, *the problem of the proletariat*, is one of cinema's original thematics. This version of the theme, which like the original focuses on female labor, is made by students from the striking cinema school. It is spring 1968, and everybody is on strike. Having voted that using their skills to document the events in flight is not strike-breaking, this will be the students' third and final film, made in the shadow of the still-unsigned Grenelle Accords through which the government and union leaders endeavored to foreclose revolution. The movie is about ten minutes long. Per the opening narration, "on the morning of June 10, 1968, after three weeks of strike and occupation of the factory, the workers of Wonder, in St-Ouen, called together by their boss, agreed to return to work, by a vote of 560 for, and 260 against." Then it introduces the action: "That same day at 1:30 . . ." The main action is this: a woman does not wish to return to work. She does not want to accede to the vote. The union functionaries from the CGT explain, placate, all with paternalistic *sang-froid*; occasionally a Maoist *etabli* looks on. The woman keeps saying *non*, shouting *non!* She does not wish to exchange the rev for the deal, absolute negation for a few more vacation days. Any fate but that of being absorbed back into the factory: "No. I'm not going back to get fucked again. I'm not going to work in there. I'm not walking back in that place. I'm not putting a foot back in that cell." But she will; we know she will.

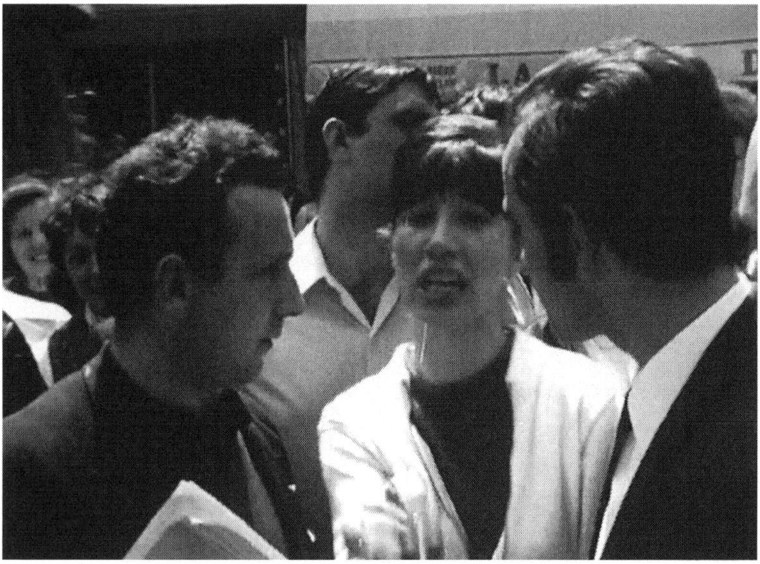

"La Reprise du travail aux usines Wonder" (1968), Jacques Willemont, Pierre Bonneau, Liane Estiez. Image captured by the author from version included in *La Reprise* (Éditions Montparnasse, 1996), Hervé Le Roux.

Decades later, for a metadocumentary called *La Reprise* (1997), a team will track down the former student filmmakers and all the people who appear in the film, except for our hero; she remains known only as "The Woman Who Says No." This is the kind of mythic shit that arises from ruptures. We don't know too much about her. She does her hair in the style of Anna Karina, as people did—Karina as she had appeared most recently in *Lo Straniero.* This is Luchino Visconti's version of Camus's *L'étranger,* finally put to film in 1967. That is a different return—in this case the return, through the cinematheque, of the Algerian decolonial war.

This is surely the other fundamental thematic of cinema that charges this moment: *the colonial problem.* What else is Méliès's *Voyage to the Moon* (1902) but the first movie about colonization? In the decade that concerns us, the most influential French documentary of the 1960s is not about 1968, though the casual investigator might believe as much from its title: Chris Marker's *Le Joli Mai* (1963). That film offers a survey of life in the metropole after the Evian Accords and Algerian independence. The two Mays, then. Two accords. *The Battle of Algiers* (1966), the most significant western representation of anticolonial warfare in the 1960s, ending with Algerian victory and thus a sort of complement to *Le Joli Mai*—the view from *Outremer*—preceded *Lo Straniero* by one year and *Return to Work at the Wonder Factory* by two. *The Battle of Algiers* was banned in France until 1970; perhaps that could be the other *non.* But no, the other *non* is within the film and within anticolonial revolution. It happens even before the beginning. An unnamed Algerian revolutionary, having been already tortured and forced humiliatingly into a French uniform, struggles miserably not to give over information about the resistance fighters. But he will; we know he will. The opening credits have not yet rolled. It is him against—hopelessly against—the French officers and the police who hector and manhandle him, perfect doubles of the union representatives from *Return to Work.* Nonetheless, he is able to offer a single excruciating *non,* to stand for a moment in the place of desperate and incomplete negation, and it is this that properly causes the film to begin, the title to appear, just as the film will end with an anti–police and military riot of the subjugated and the colonized, the social *non* that will end in Algerian liberation.

The Battle of Algiers (1966), Gillo Pontecorvo. Image captured by the author from Criterion edition (2004).

So these are the two *non*s with which I begin—the two nameless characters, the two hands on the shoulder, the two iterations of *allons-y*, "let's go," the two parallel yet utterly distinct modes of domination. I want to note, as to continue this procedure of lining up an extended series of imperfect pairings, and as a matter of being attentive to the place where this essay was first presented, that we might see in these two frameworks a relation to the particularities of Milwaukee, its history, its present organization. Milwaukee was the first city in the United States to have a socialist mayor, to send a socialist representative to Congress. It is also the most segregated city in the nation at the time of this writing, with the highest Black employment, a basis for the riots here in 2016. These two features offer a local reflection on the two cinematic problems raised earlier, *the problem of the proletariat and the colonial problem*. But I take that phrase from elsewhere.

"The fact is that so-called European civilization—'Western' civilization—as it has been shaped by two centuries of bourgeois rule," writes Aimé Césaire in his *Discourse on Colonialism* (originally published in 1955), "is incapable of solving the two major problems to which its existence has given rise: the problem of the proletariat and the colonial problem."[2] What I want to suggest is that these two problems, while remaining distinct, disclose a conceptual unity in the fact and figure of the surplus population, surplus to capital and its needs and thus legible only incompletely within its logic, negatively legible, legible through NO.

Recent discussions of surplus population generally understand its historical increase, detailed by Mike Davis, Jan Bremen, Jacques Charmes, and others, as a consequence of capitalist development. Stagnant surplus populations are the specter waiting at the conclusion of Marx's extended logical argument in *Capital Volume 1*, in chapter 25, before the book leaps sideways into history. The crisis character of capital driven by compulsory increases in productivity manifests itself in what is best understood as *the production of nonproduction*: excess capacity and excess labor stacked cheek by jowl with no rationale by which they might be brought together, at least not within capital's logic. It is requisite to note that this deference toward the category of productivity is not mine (or Marx's) but is enforced by capital itself, which exists to the precise degree that it produces surplus value.

Accepting this account, I want nonetheless to approach the problems—Césaire's two problems—somewhat differently, by presupposing that we can refigure the abstract negation that is nonproduction toward more concrete social actors and restate matters thusly: the *threat of surplus population* is immanent to the bourgeois era. In turn I suggest that strategies for managing this threat help constitute different regimes of politics and distinct views about revolutionary actors. I do not mean simply to taxonomize, however, but to attend to a striking fact of our era, which is the convergence of these two regimes.

My title pairing, "absorption and coloniality," names the two regimes of managing surplus but risks misreading. At least initially, this essay may seem to set these two regimes against each other, one under the name of Marx and one under the name of Fanon; consequently, it may appear, particularly in our moment, that this is an intervention into debates about, if not the priority of one or the other, at least the distinct characters of capitalism or colonialism as a master term for understanding the historical dynamic that has most ambitiously and fatally organized the globe. Even worse, it may seem to offer a reductive opposition of race and class of the sort that has burst forth anew in the wake of recent hypertrophied nativism in the White House entangled with the asymmetrical rise of xenophobic nationalism and social democratic populism. As I hope will become clear, this is not the case, though I will take Césaire at his word that there is such a thing as "two centuries of bourgeois rule," within which his two problems increasingly take their significance.

One might also suspect that I am adopting the term *coloniality* from Aníbal Quijano in his well-known essays on the coloniality of power, in which the term designates an ensemble of characteristics, weighted toward the epistemological, that define in the first instance the relation of Europe and Latin America developed well in advance of Césaire's two centuries. This confusion can, I hope, be avoided. I am using it instead to refer to the mode of social organization and management explored by Fanon, particularly in *Wretched of the Earth*. As will, I hope, become clear, I use *coloniality* rather than *colonialism* simply to distinguish it as a substantive approach to domination rather than as a given national order—as a global political project and ideology, such that we can think of *instances* of coloniality at various scales, including the domestic and local, though no doubt the nation-state has been the form through which coloniality has been most dramatically imposed *as* colonialism and whose existence has most depended on the violence of coloniality.

The character of this violence is in some degree what is at stake in the distinction between, and unity of, absorption and coloniality. Coloniality has depended on racialized and racializing hierarchies that institute and enforce subordination through the direct domination of the whip and the wall, the pass card and the prison, delivered differentially to discipline unfree labor, expropriate land and resources, and maintain exclusions. Such a framework cuts against the grain of the great exceptionalism that allows chattel slavery in particular as it developed in the United States after 1619 to provide an ordering principle for domination in general at a global scale, and thus allows for seeing social relation rather than ontological difference between, for example, formerly enslaved and indigenous populations in North America, while seeing in turn their relation to the colonization studied by Fanon, all of these distinct from and entangled with the orientation toward wage discipline of free labor that characterizes absorptive regimes.

Among the differences between Marx and Fanon, the great analysts of absorption and coloniality, their visions of revolutionary subjects, stand in dramatic opposition, opposed neatly by their assessments of the status of the lumpenproletariat, those decisively rather than momentarily outside the formal wage. Surely all remember the macaronic litany in the *Eighteenth Brumaire*: "vagabonds, discharged soldiers, discharged jailbirds, escaped galley slaves, swindlers, mountebanks, lazzaroni, pickpockets, tricksters, gamblers, *maquereaux*, brothel keepers, porters, literati, organ grinders, ragpickers, knife grinders, tinkers, beggars—in short, the whole indefinite, disintegrated mass," as Marx says, a concatenation without doubt counterrevolutionary, subject to the sway of whoever held the day, notably Bonaparte, "chief of the Paris lumpen proletariat."[3]

For Fanon, the matter appears contrarily. "These men," he writes,

> forced off the family land by the growing population in the countryside and by colonial expropriation, circle the towns tirelessly, hoping that one day or another they will be let in. It is among these masses, in the people of the shanty towns and in the lumpenproletariat that the insurrection will find its urban spearhead. The lumpenproletariat, this cohort of starving men, divorced from tribe and clan, constitutes one of the most spontaneously and radically revolutionary forces of a colonized people.[4]

Lest we think he is talking about some other social fraction, he conjures Marx's litany immediately thereafter: "So the pimps, the hooligans, the unemployed, and the petty criminals, when approached, give the liberation struggle all they have got, devoting themselves to the cause like valiant workers."[5] It is hard not to understand that concluding simile as a specific demand on Marx, or on orthodox Marxism, to understand this surplus population as party of an expanded proletariat, as class revolutionaries.

In "Reading Fanon in the 21st Century," Wallerstein points us to the salience of this debate: "Aimé Césaire's *Discourse on Colonialism* remains the classic expression of why intellectuals of the colonial world (and of course not they alone) withdrew their commitment to Communist parties and asserted a revised version of the class struggle. The key issue in these debates was the question, which are the classes that are struggling?" Having set forth this debate, he warns us not to make too much of Fanon's contribution. "There were many proposals of new candidates for the historical subject who would be the 'spearhead' of revolutionary activity," he notes. "Fanon thought he had located them in the detribalized, urbanized, lumpenproletariat. But he admitted his doubts when he depicted the 'pitfalls of spontaneity.'"[6]

This much is true; Fanon understands the lumpen insurrection as a moment that must transform toward broader struggle, not as itself the revolution entire. Yet, in his curiously bifurcated rebuttal, Wallerstein restates Fanon in moralizing terms ("violence, however therapeutic and however effective, solves nothing"), while reorienting Fanon's argument back toward an orthodoxy it would not recognize: "lumpen-classes, on their own, without organizational structure, burn out."[7] We might on another occasion wonder if there is a subterranean current joining orthodoxy and moralism. For the moment, rather than choosing a side, I want only to pursue the basis of this seeming disagreement between Marx and Fanon.

To state matters as clearly as possible: for all of Marx's contempt and Fanon's optimism, their divergence does not rest on some *variation of opinion* about the essential character of the lumpen, much less some moral stance. Nor need it be the case that one must be correct, the other mistaken. Choosing a side in this debate is to miss its historically concrete character. Rather, we might say that the lumpenproletariat, if the term is capable of designating a comparable tranche of the proletariat across time and space—and I think it is—has a different position in the metropole in 1850 than in the colony a century later. The former is characterized overall by dynamism, by the rude expansion of adolescent capital on the march, and in turn by the impersonal domination of the wage, whose grace, it was supposed, would fall on more people each year, calling out even to the Society of December 10 and seeming to put on offer to them the opportunity to pluck the fruits of capital's largesse—the Society who felt, in Marx's words, "the need of benefiting themselves at the expense of the laboring nation." The latter is characterized by a peculiar motion, one whose truth is the real stasis of "a world compartmentalized, Manichaean and petrified, a world of statues: the statue of the general the statue of the engineer who built the bridge."[8] For Fanon, "the colonial subject is a man penned in; apartheid is but one method of compartmentalizing the colonial world."[9] In this situation, "the lumpenproletariat constitutes a serious threat to the 'security' of the town and signifies the irreversible rot and the gangrene eating into the heart of colonial domination."[10] Colonial rule is securitization. This security threat, this absolute proscription on any kind of integration, the racialized proscription that constitutes the colonized, will not be—*cannot be*—managed in main by wage discipline, which is the social form of integration. It will be managed rather by direct domination: "The colonized world is a world divided in two. The dividing line, the border, is represented by the barracks and the police stations. In the colonies, the official, legitimate agent, the spokesperson for the colonizer and the regime of oppression, is the police officer or the soldier."[11] This is a way of understanding, among other things, that the colonial relation—even from a Marxist standpoint—must be understood as featuring not just subjugated, unfree labor compelled by the lash but subjugated, unfree *nonlabor*. That may be our third and secret *non* that unites the first two.

We see, then, the distinct solutions to Césaire's two problems of the proletarian in the metropole and the excluded in the colony, two forms of threatening surplus. One solution is economic expansion, the capacity to take that surplus population into the circuits of value production and accumulation, the thematic that Lukács, in discussing the eighteenth- and nineteenth-century novel, names as "reconciliation." This is the regime that I am calling *absorption*. The other is open and immanent violence directed against those for whom every doorway is labeled NO ENTRY, in a colonial world itself forever labeled NO EXIT. This is the regime I am calling *coloniality*.

The opposition should not be exaggerated. It is, in truth, not an opposition at all. Both absorption and coloniality feature

Manichaean racialized domination and the regulatory compulsions of value production. Perhaps we are speaking of a relatively unitary *colonial capitalism*, there being no other kind.[12] Or *capitalist colonization*. There may nonetheless be a certain yield to drawing the distinction, to noting the differing orientations of these two regimes. While the former features and arguably depends on racialized exclusion, on moments of internal colonization, and indeed, as Marx notes, "the veiled slavery of the wageworkers in Europe needed, for its pedestal, slavery pure and simple in the new world," this is subordinated to capital's self-expansion and intensification at the scale of national economy.[13] While the latter is subject to the constraints of global capitalist relations, it is not an absorptive capitalism, at least not absorptive enough to challenge what Fanon insists is the historical speciation that divides colonizer and colonized. And it is *from within these two regimes*, absorption and coloniality, that the lumpen appear differently: here as counterrevolutionary dregs, here as revolutionary edge.

If one accepts, implicitly or openly, the premise of ongoing accumulation at a global scale (a presupposition not just for capital but for purported antagonists, notably the majority of socialist parties new and old), the assumption is that the unevenness between these two regimes will smooth over time. This has proved to be the case. However, it has not happened in the way foreseen either by orthodox Marxism or by the apostles of capital. While the so-called underdeveloped nations have in moments crept or leapt forward, the developed nations have become overdeveloped in ways that have effectively moved them back toward a political economy that is, if not technically colonial (an unresolved technicality), *nonabsorptive in a way that functionally replicates coloniality*: a regime in which any desire for reconciliation with the circuits of value production cannot be met, where more and more people globally find themselves circling the towns, never to be granted admission. This is our present. Increasing productivity has led these nations through peak labor force participation as sectors expand behind high profit rates and then toward a deindustrialization in which ever-higher productivity no longer implies an extension of the wage, leaving both an absolute and a relative increase of population consigned to the informal economy. It is the technical category of informalization that Marx is setting forth in his great litany: those for whom secondary access to the wage provides the only hope of survival in the form of petty production, gray market recirculation, and so on. What Marx did not envision was the growth of this sector until it provided no longer the lower margin of a class, a provisional congeries drifting in and out of the labor pool, but a class fragment itself, truly stagnant and simply excluded—an exclusion conducted historically along logics of race and ethnicity that both recapitulate and reproduce racial ascription.

It is precisely this drama that animates efforts to understand the relation of U.S. ghettos to colonies abroad: the so-called internal colonies thesis that dates back to the Black Belt Republic of Harry Haywood and others in the Communist Party USA but takes on a new and different force in the 1960s as deindustrialization begins. This thinking depends only partially on an analogy between domestic and global colonization. In the formulations of, for example, Huey P. Newton, he feels compelled to discover the political economy of social death. The situation is ambiguous, heterogeneous—as is racial capitalism in its truest form. Trying to grasp the situation, Newton contradicts himself. On one side, Black populations are ruthlessly *exploited* to deliver superprofits necessary for imperial adventures. "The slavery of Blacks in this country provides the oil for the machinery of war that America uses to enslave the world," he writes.[14] On the other, Black populations are *excluded*; from about 1960 onward, a racialized deindustrialization starts to take hold in the cities of the second great migration. Consequently, "penned up in the ghettoes of America, surrounded by all his factories and all the physical components of his economic system, we have been made into 'the wretched of the earth,' relegated to the position of spectators."[15] Black lumpen, catastrophically free of wage discipline, must in turn be managed by "the occupying army, embodied by the police department."[16] The echoes of Fanon's "colonial world" are unmistakable.

This exclusion is registered even earlier by the prescient James Boggs, circa 1963, the year of *Wretched*'s translation into English: "Today in the United States there is no doubt that those at the bottom are growing in numbers much faster than the system will ever be able to absorb," he suggests, concluding that "America is headed toward full unemployment, not full employment."[17] Those who do find work are trapped in a job market so intensely polarized that there can be no escape imagined from poverty. Meanwhile, those surplus to the needs of capital and empire grow, and grow restless. Boggs's Detroit in the years following would be defined by the intersection of absorption struggles and risings against coloniality, by the League of Revolutionary Black Workers and the Great Rebellion whose fiftieth anniversary we marked in summer 2017. It is 1967, the same year as Newton's double-exposure of the ghetto, the same moment as our two initial *nons*.

My argument, if it has not yet become clear, is that Newton's contradiction, or Detroit's, is not a paradox, not a sign of inadequate analysis, but the registration of a transformation in flight. These instances figure *coloniality within absorption*, or one might say instead, refiguring the same phenomenon, *neocoloniality's emergence*, as the capacity for absorption wanes in the face of irresolvable crisis. One signal account of this transition is surely that of Ruth Wilson Gilmore, who identifies racialized hyperincarceration incisively within a context of crisis and surplus. This state management of surplus, articulated within a logic of domestic securitization against urban threat, whose "official, legitimate agent, the spokesperson for the colonizer and the regime of oppression, is the police officer or the soldier," to recall Fanon's terms, is precisely how I have defined coloniality.[18] Another is *Policing the Crisis* by Stuart Hall and his comrades (the text in which Hall first tests out his repeated formula "race is the modality through which class is lived"). In both cases, we can follow fairly close and empirical studies of the ways that surplus populations both raced not-white and classed as lumpen, in train of broad economic collapse beginning in the 1960s from which there has been no substantive recovery, are disciplined increasingly via direct domination.

This is the most distressing evocation of the oceanic change in question: a global recomposition of social relations. It is this historical change for which we must account. The *allons-y* of the colonel converges with that of the union rep. Indeed, and this aspect of the argument will have to be developed elsewhere, we might see the *non* of our nameless woman as the collapse of the workers' movements in the West, as unions devolve into purely defensive struggles and the declining absorption of the labor markets leaves a slack that destroys workers' bargaining power even as it undermines profitability of firms. It is a *non* to that manner of labor struggle. From this point on, the class-mass party sequence leading to seizure of state power and a transitional program toward socialist ownership recedes from the revolutionary horizon; the program era is over. But something else is beginning. Or something is returning, utterly changed, as is the way with the new. In this transformed circumstance, the Big No is no longer an impossible demand, a subjective cry. After absorption's end, it is a recognition of the objective circumstance as it must be lived.

Which is to say that we find ourselves, here, now, in a world closer to that of Fanon than of Marx. The United States is the greatest absorptive regime the world has ever known, and the most self-regarding. You can tell because this is the nation's motto. It is written in huge letters on the Statue of Liberty, the nation's very own poem: WELCOME TO THE WORLD CAPITAL OF ABSORPTION. I am paraphrasing, but not much. This is what has come to an end. New York offers a convenient periodization for the United States: during the 1977 blackout, when the entire power grid failed for twenty-five hours, only the torch on the Statue of Liberty stayed lit, having a separate power source. By the time of Superstorm Sandy in 2012, famously, the only lights in downtown Manhattan belonged to a single corporate headquarters, with their autonomous generator—Goldman Sachs, the earthly representative of profit without accumulation, wealth without absorption. It is possible, I suppose, to read this change nostalgically, to prefer the torch of liberty to the luminous options grifters. No, both are worse. The lights are beaming wonders, but history is with the blackout.

This turn toward a greater rather than lesser coloniality, ever more oriented not by left–right debates within a liberal–democratic framework but by the axis of inclusion and exclusion, is the basis among other things for Black Lives Matter, the resurgence of what I elsewhere call "surplus rebellions" or urban and suburban rioting, and for a renewed nativist code of hyperracism and protectionism.[19] When we think of Trump's accession in 2016, we might understand it as an experiment in management style for the end of absorption.

This broader phenomenon, the end of absorption and the arrival of the colony to the metropole, is no less marked in Europe—indeed, it is the continental story, from Brexit to the refugee crisis to the slow dissolution of the European Union, three entangled phenomena. The debate over borders and their ongoing closure may appear as xenophobia, and no doubt it is; its power and its salience are driven no less by the European Economic Community's ongoing stagnation, a continental zero-sum economic game that has enriched Germany and to some extent the Netherlands at the expense of the Europeriphery, with France holding even. Zero sum, end of absorption, same difference. And so Fortress Europe is now the town Fanon mentions, around which the global lumpen circle, hoping that, one day or another, they will be allowed inside. Even this dire achievement is not on offer.

So then, some summary remarks. One, disclosed along the way. Liberal democracy, the kind with a left and a right, not long ago thought to have generalized itself so thoroughly that history had ended, is waning. It is not waning because it is being overdone by the rapacity of capitalism but *because it is absorptive capitalism's management style and must decline with it.* Alexis de Tocqueville saw the entanglement of liberal rights and dynamic labor markets early on: "Equality not only ennobles the idea of work itself but also enhances it, even if it is for money. . . . But in democratic societies, these two ideas [work and profit] are always visibly linked. . . . As soon as work seems to all citizens an honorable necessity for the human race and is always clearly performed, at least in part, for payment, then the wide gap which used to separate the different professions in aristocratic societies disappears. If they are not exactly similar, at least they share a common characteristic."[20]

Two, thereby, the United States and Europe, the "developed nations," capital's home countries, are overdeveloping toward a weaponized mode of inclusion/exclusion against and by which the planetary *classes dangereuses* are increasingly united, not by their role as producers, but by their relation to state violence. Consequently, the informalized, the surplus population, takes on Fanon's revolutionary aspect more broadly. The *non* of Paris is not simply the dialectical other of the Algerian *non* but increasingly must become it.

Three, this risks setting the excluded *against* the working class that still exists as a sociological fact central to the imaginary of various contemporary social democratic visions, occasionally under the heading of the "white working class." This imaginary, despite occasional and sometimes indifferent lip service to racialized exclusion, retains a world picture of social reorganization derived entirely from the expansivity of absorptive capital and the organizational protocols that accompanied that capacity for absorption. There are still so-called leftists who think we can grow ourselves out of trouble, or who turn a blind eye to the global subordinations on which the wealth for progammatic social spending rests.

Or four, we will develop an expanded sense of a global proletariat as a historical phenomenon premised in a shifting set of relations, open to and indeed unable to escape transformations, which in the present discovers the potential for a new unity of lumpen and labor, allowed precisely by the weakening of intraclass competition that follows, dripping immiseration, from the end of absorption.

If there is to be a revolutionary project, it will resemble decolonization, not in the sense of nationalist armed struggle against a colonial state but as a struggle against a capitalism *compelled to act as colonial*. These are the coordinates toward which a potential recomposition of class power might orient itself and find its own historical significance. It will not be orderly in the ways imagined by the prophets of revolutionary projects preserved from the previous century. Like Fanon's decolonization, this revolution, "which sets out to change the order of the world, is, obviously, a program of complete disorder."[21]

As a final gesture, we might consider one of the early efforts of conceptualizing the leap of this manner of antagonism to the metropole, in Sam Greenlee's epochal *The Spook Who Sat by the Door*. The book takes as its fundamental problematic the question of how riot can become revolution. For Greenlee, writing in the late 1960s (the book was published in 1969), it is precisely the presence of Black surplus population gathered in U.S. ghettos that provides the conditions of possibility for such a leap: "Oakland blew first, then Los Angeles, then, leap-frogging the continent, Harlem and South Philadelphia. . . . Every city with a ghetto wondered if they might be next. The most powerful nation in history stood on the brink of panic and chaos."[22] Two, three, many Casbahs. In an eloquent dialectical turn, it is precisely the *technē* of global repression, the state's investment in preserving its imperial aspirations, that provides for the success of this war against the state, owing to our titular hero's skills acquired as the token Black officer with the CIA, distributed to a network of the informalized, the wageless, gamblers, *maquereaux*, brothel keepers, porters, possibly even literati. Counterinsurgency and securitization at a global level return as insurgency and threat in the urban cores, hollowed by development itself.

It is hard to say that history's NO will unfold in precisely this manner; it is certain that there will be no return to work at the wonder factory.

Notes

1. This essay is a sort of experiment in concatenation. It began as little more than an intuition during a centenary roundtable for *Theory of the Novel* and develops ideas toward an as-yet-entitled assessment of the geopolitical economy of the world system as it makes its fateful turn away from U.S.-centered accumulation and perhaps away from capitalism as we have known it. Be that as it may, this version takes up an earlier, briefer version of the main argument designated in the title ("Fanon: Absorption and Coloniality," *College Literature* 45, no. 1 [2018]: 39–45) and begins to add to it these moments of cultural production in which an ongoing global change is registered cinematically. The essay will no doubt develop further in further iterations. I am grateful to the Center for 21st Century Studies at the University of Wisconsin–Milwaukee and to the thoughtful organizers of the conference where this material was first presented, especially Kennan Ferguson.
2. Aimé Césaire, *Discourse on Colonialism*, trans. Joan Pinkham (1955; repr., New York: Monthly Review Press, 1972), 1.
3. Karl Marx, *The Class Struggles in France: From the February Revolution to the Paris Commune* (Chippendale, Australia: Resistance Books, 2003), 170–71.
4. Frantz Fanon, *The Wretched of the Earth*, trans. Richard Philcox (1963; repr., New York: Grove Press, 2004), 81.

5. Marx, 81–82.
6. Immanuel Wallerstein, "Reading Fanon in the 21st Century," *New Left Review* 57 (May–June 2009): 124.
7. Wallerstein, 125.
8. Fanon, 15.
9. Fanon.
10. Fanon, 81.
11. Fanon, 3.
12. Glen Sean Coulthard uses the term *settler capitalism* in trying to understand the political economy of what is now Canada; it is a useful and portable formulation.
13. Karl Marx, *Capital Volume 1*, trans. Ben Fowkes (1867; repr., New York: Vintage, 1967), 925.
14. Huey P. Newton, *The Huey P. Newton Reader*, ed. David Hilliard and Donald Weise (New York: Seven Stories Press, 2011), 136.
15. Newton.
16. Newton, 149.
17. James Boggs, *Pages from a Black Radical's Notebook: A James Boggs Reader* (Detroit, Mich.: Wayne State University Press, 2011), 112, 118.
18. Fanon, *Wretched of the Earth*, 3.
19. Joshua Clover, *Riot.Strike.Riot: The New Era of Uprisings* (New York: Verso, 2016), 152.
20. Alexis de Tocqueville, *Democracy in America*, trans. and ed. Harvey C. Mansfield and Delba Winthrop (1835; repr., Chicago: University of Chicago Press, 2002), 525–26.
21. Fanon, *Wretched of the Earth*, 2.
22. Sam Greenlee, *The Spook Who Sat by the Door* (Detroit, Mich.: Wayne State University Press, 1969), 236.

2
Antisocial (A Literary History)

Theodore Martin

> There is no phenomenon [. . .] which does not take place *in* society.
>
> —*Émile Durkheim*

Is there such a thing as society? Scholars across the disciplines are becoming increasingly comfortable with the idea that there isn't. "What if," the literary critic David Alworth wonders approvingly, "there is no such thing as society?"[1] If the claim that society does not exist once called to mind the austere neoliberalism of Margaret Thatcher, today it is more likely to invoke the iconoclastic sociology of Bruno Latour, for whom "there is no social dimension of any sort, no 'social context,' no distinct domain of reality to which the label 'social' or 'society' could be attributed."[2] Associations, not totalization: this is the bedrock of a Latourian "school of thought" that Latour himself admits "could use as its slogan what Mrs. Thatcher famously exclaimed (but for very different reasons!)."[3] With Latour's actor-network-theory, Thatcher's neoliberal slogan appears to have been raised to the level of methodological principle.[4] This principle insists that there are flexible networks, temporary affiliations, weak ties—but there is no such thing as *society*. That particular term, these critics suggest, is a meaningless abstraction, if not a misleading fiction.

Is society really so debased a concept? In one sense, the charges against it are true. Society *doesn't* exist—if what you mean by society is an object whose existence can be measured, quantified, or empirically confirmed. This is what someone like Rita Felski seems to mean when she suggests that "the social just is the act and the fact of association." For Felski, there is no "shadowy," ineffable society that lies "behind [. . .] human practices"; there are just those concrete human (and, she would probably add, nonhuman) practices.[5] Felski, Latour, and others present their debunking of the myth of society as a new and necessary corrective to decades of ossified thinking about social determination. In fact, it is not so new. More than a century ago, the sociologist Émile Durkheim sought to refute exactly the claim that Latour and Felski make today: the claim that society is nothing but "a mental construct, a metaphysical entity which the scholar can and must neglect [. . .] a composite in which there is nothing more than the sum of its components."[6] At the time Durkheim was writing, this claim was associated with the discipline of mainstream economics, which sought to reduce the "metaphysical entity" of society down to the acts and associations of so many individual *homines oeconomici*. As Durkheim saw it, it was a mistake to think of society as just the acts and facts of individuals and their associations. What such a view failed to acknowledge were the "ways of acting, thinking, and feeling that present the remarkable property of existing outside the individual consciousness." These "collective habits," no matter how remarkable in their apparent disembodiment, nonetheless "find expression in definite forms: legal rules, moral regulations, popular proverbs, social conventions."[7] It is this feedback loop of collective habits and institutional forms that points to an entity that "exist[s] outside" the material fact of individuals. The term for that entity is *society*: at once the end product and the governing process of human lives lived in the plural. And as Durkheim reminded his readers a century ago, the fact that we can't see it does not constitute sufficient proof that it does not exist.

In what follows, my attempt to intervene in current debates about the critical value of the concept of society takes the form less of a theoretical argument than of a literary-historical inquiry: what has it meant at different moments for novelists to suggest that society doesn't exist, and how has that suggestion been recorded by literary form? Across the nineteenth and twentieth centuries, the form of the novel was persistently torn between the desire for social withdrawal and the force of the social whole. Yet the literary history of these dueling impulses is hardly a static one. Rather, such a history helps us see how the imaginative uses of antisociality changed over time. What began as a pleasurable fantasy of social escape, I'll argue, would soon become a violent record of the very inescapability of social determination.[8]

To be sure, the novel is at once a profoundly social literary form and a peculiarly antisocial one. Historians and theorists of the novel have long insisted on the novel's defining social uses: its instruction in sympathy, its teaching of economic credibility, its articulation of invisible community.[9] Yet there is a well-known antisocial side to the novel as well: it narrates public life, yet shores up private property; it depicts social interaction, yet affirms the primacy of interiority;[10] it teaches us sympathy, but only in sessions of private reading;[11] most of all, it guarantees its own special social status only by inventing a category—fiction—that is defined first and foremost as the formal opposite of the social world.[12] These constitutive antisocial elements—the solitude of reading, the priority of privacy, and the extrasocial status of fiction itself—suggest a kind of shadow history of the modern novel. This is a history in which the novel form turns out to be less a lesson in empathy or identification than a way of grappling with a series of escalating contradictions that lie at the heart of both social life and literary form: the contradiction between ourselves and other people, between the concreteness of other people and the abstraction of society, and finally between society and literature—which is to say, between what we take to be the real world and what we are capable of imagining as alternatives to it.

The history of sociality and the literary history of antisociality have recently garnered a fair share of critical attention in the context of nineteenth-century Britain. In an era shaped by the birth of social science, by the new dominance of an industrialized market economy, by unprecedented levels of social density, and by what D. A. Miller famously called "the emergence of [. . .] modern disciplinary power in general," nineteenth-century British novels frequently sought both to map the scope of the social system and to imagine some (purely fictional) escape from it.[13] As

Jeff Nunokawa points out, "people go to considerable lengths to get away from others in the nineteenth-century novel, and to get others away from them."[14] There are different ways of understanding the nineteenth-century inclination toward social withdrawal. Christopher Lane, for one, emphasizes the deep vein of misanthropy running through the period. Exemplified by Oscar Wilde's well-known quip that "the only possible society is oneself," Victorian culture, Lane suggests, gave "antisocial behavior a thrilling, if vicarious, appeal."[15] In doing so, nineteenth-century literature taught readers "whom to hate, and what [to] do with that emotion."[16] Gage McWeeny notices the same "weak forms of sociality, or even apparent antisociality," shaping the Victorian novel. But he sees the period's representative "antisocial sociability" as having a more positive function for British culture. "Social detachment," in McWeeny's account, ironically expresses not hatred or rejection but a "yearning toward collective social life."[17]

For Lane, Victorian antisociality reveals the inhospitable and unneighborly feelings lying behind the facade of British sociability; for McWeeny, that same antisociality bespeaks the desire for an abstract, impersonal collectivity located beyond domestic intimacy. But if Lane and McWeeny disagree on the precise connotations of antisocial sentiment, they nevertheless agree that such sentiment emerged as a challenge to the Victorian era's compulsory forms of sociality. For both critics, the nineteenth-century antisocial novel represents a fictional counterpoint to the historical emergence of modern society—a society that was densely populated, tightly regulated, highly conventionalized, and consolidated into an object of both literary and scientific study. Under those historical conditions, literary depictions of escaping from society were as necessary as they were imaginary. Put differently, such escapes were constitutively novelistic. The Victorian antisocial novel existed in dialectical relation to the compulsion of social belonging and the perceived force of social regulation. The possibility of getting away from other people appeared in so many nineteenth-century novels precisely because it wasn't felt to exist in nineteenth-century society itself.

The story of the antisocial novel in nineteenth-century Britain, then, is a story about the sometimes unbearable feeling of ineluctable sociality. Over the course of the twentieth century, however, antisocial fiction began to tell a rather different story—one about the gradual fraying of social bonds and the apparent disintegration of the social whole. In the United States today, this is a story that most commonly appears under the title *neoliberalism* and whose most frequently cited chapters include stagnating wages, rising unemployment, increased inequality, and the concerted dismantling of the welfare state. Most readers will be familiar with how the rise of austerity politics has played out in the twenty-first century. Many will further recognize that these are processes that began in earnest several decades ago, with the twin assaults on social welfare and organized labor that entered the political mainstream in the 1980s. Yet to grasp the full scope of our contemporary epoch of antisocial social relations, it is necessary to begin still earlier in the twentieth century—not with Thatcher and Reagan but with the crisis of the liberal state that, in the wake of World War II, reshaped American conceptions of social responsibility and the common good.[18]

One of the most intractable puzzles of midcentury U.S. history has been how the "proto-social democracy" of the New Deal broke apart in the 1940s and 1950s.[19] In the postwar years, New Deal aspirations toward social democracy and wealth redistribution ran aground on the transformed ideological framework, policy imperatives, and material conditions of the incipient Cold War. Emergent suspicions about the role of the federal government manifested both in liberal reconciliation with the free market and in the conservative push for government collaborations with private industry. This ideological convergence had a profound impact on American social life. Public policy became narrowly focused on promoting growth and boosting consumption; welfare was privatized (in the form of benefits tied to employment, for example); and images of American freedom and individualism—emblematized in the classic figure of the teenage rebel[20]—were used to ward off the ostensibly deadening force of Soviet-style central planning. Viewed through the lens of these epochal social and political changes, a midcentury era generally associated with conformity and consensus turns out to be the decisive period in which the commitments to social welfare and economic equality were replaced by bipartisan allegiance to privatization, deregulation, and individual consumption.

As the historian Ira Katznelson argues, the dissolution of the New Deal order during and after the war "changed the locus of political debate from questions of social organization and class relations to issues of technical economics and interest group politics."[21] With this shift of focus, the New Deal principles of economic equality and a strong regulatory state gave way to the alienation and anomie of a new postwar consumer society, one whose ideological sense of abundance and celebration of choice dramatically weakened support for social welfare while making class solidarity appear, in the face of such apparent prosperity, all but unnecessary.[22] The decisive turn away from "macroeconomic planning and social welfare goals"[23] in the midcentury United States cast into new and radical doubt the ideals of social welfare and shared responsibility that had shaped the major achievements of the New Deal. The abandonment of social and economic planning in the 1940s signaled a major shift in liberal thought in the period. Whereas New Deal liberals had insisted that the structural inequities of a capitalist economy could only be managed by a strong state, postwar liberals made peace with a capitalist system that was visibly booming during and after the war. With this about-face, the collectivist, state-centered vision of society that briefly entered American public life in the 1930s was displaced by an unapologetically capitalist, consumerist, and individualist worldview. As Alan Brinkley argues,

> by 1945, the wartime experience had led most to conclude [. . .] that neither a new economic order nor active state management of the present one were necessary, possible, or even desirable; that the existing structure of capitalism (including its relative independence from state control) was the best hope for social progress; and that the government's most important task was less to regulate the private economy than to help it expand and to compensate for its occasional failures.[24]

The incontrovertible evidence of capitalist success supplied by the postwar boom helped transform the period's political ideology.

As the historian Carol A. Horton explains, "growing prosperity widely discredited the progressive position that it was important to have socially directed governmental interference in the capitalist market." In short, by the end of the 1940s, "the achievement of a booming consumer economy [. . .] replaced the vision of a more equitable society."[25]

The upheavals of the postwar years—including the economic boom, the rise of the suburbs, the diminished horizons of the labor movement, and increasingly undeniable evidence of the country's constitutive racial violence—can, in a sense, be said to have remade the very idea of society as it circulated in American discourse. As the political scientist Theodore Lowi argued in 1969, the postwar social order was built on a newly institutionalized "dread of such poetic terms as 'public interest,' 'the state,' and 'sovereignty.' "[26] Katznelson concurs; the post–New Deal social order, he suggests, institutionalized a growing disinclination to consider social and economic problems in terms of a larger "social totality." Rather than attempting to make sense of the complex and shifting nature of society, public policy was now dominated by a version of neoclassical economics that considered economic problems in isolation from social ones. The new dominance of professional economists in the arena of public policy meant that, in Katznelson's words, "social organization and human nature were now to be taken as givens."[27] In particular, what was now taken as a given was the very idea that Durkheim had sought to debunk half a century before: that "society" was nothing but an aggregate of isolated, individual economic actors. On this view, there were neither structural problems nor systemic solutions; in fact, very little about the world could be understood as shared at all. With social and political problems successfully retranslated into the language of economic (and specifically microeconomic) theory, social life in postwar America came to be dominated by what Annie McClanahan calls, in her cultural history of microeconomics, a kind of "philosophical antisociality," a philosophy that served to authorize the "ostensibly virtuous rejection of the very idea of society."[28]

This newly antisocial moment in American history—a moment that marked a radical rethinking of the relation between individuals and the construct we call society—created the conditions for a new kind of antisocial novel. The particular antisocial slant of midcentury American literature is captured by one of the era's most distinctive literary creations: the criminal sociopath. As Sean McCann explains in his history of American crime fiction, the paperback originals of the 1950s "remade the hard-boiled [detective] story into a drama of psychopathology" whose "typical protagonist became a freak, a loser, or a sociopath."[29] Leonard Cassuto likewise views the 1950s as a key moment in the invention of "nonconformist crime fiction," a genre style that sought to "inhabit the twisted minds of the transgressors."[30] Eschewing the law-abiding and order-restoring work associated with the canonical character of the detective, many midcentury crime writers began instead to explore the literary affordances of the sympathetic sociopath. They did so, I argue in the remainder of this essay, as a way to come to terms with the new antisocial dynamics of their time.

"Criminality," write the anthropologists Jean and John Comaroff, channeling Durkheim, "is a critical prism by means of which societies know themselves."[31] In the case of midcentury American fiction, we can go one step further and think of criminality as the prism through which writers attempted to determine whether society—a collection of social imperatives that, in Durkheim's words, are "external to the individual"—could actually be said to exist in the first place. The literary sociopath's rejection not only of social norms but, as we shall see, of the very idea of society captures in microcosm what Erving Goffman would diagnose in his 1963 book *Stigma* as the "collective denial of the social order."[32] This collective refusal—its feasibility, its effects, and, finally, its contradictions—was the main subject of the midcentury antisocial novel. The character of the criminal sociopath offered a uniquely apt literary test case for deciding, are we governed by a shared sense of social ties, or are we ruled, paradoxically, by nothing but our shared denial of them?

Who Is Society?

One of the great antisocial moments in American literature comes at the end of Patricia Highsmith's 1950 crime novel *Strangers on a Train*. In the novel's final scene, the tormented protagonist Guy

Haines—who, after a chance encounter on a train with the sociopath Charles Bruno, is implicated in two separate killings—attempts to confess his crimes to a stranger. But Guy discovers something strange: the stranger doesn't care.

> "What business is it of mine?" [Owen] asked firmly.
> "What business? Because you—you are a part of society!"
> "Well, then it's society's business," Owen replied with a lazy wave of his hand.
> What business, Guy thought. Was that his real attitude, or was he drunk? It must be Owen's attitude. . . . Then he remembered it had been his own attitude. . . . Was this most people's attitude? If so, who was society?[33]

Society, Guy discovers, is made up of people who don't believe in society. Society's abstraction in the form of what Guy will later call "inexorable rules" is something that everyone assumes everyone else is responsible for policing but that no one feels responsible for themself. With this realization, Guy is led to ask himself, "Would Brillhart [his former boss] have reported him? No. He couldn't imagine Brillhart reporting him. Everyone would leave it for someone else, who would leave it for someone else, who would leave it for someone else, and no one would do it."[34] The irony woven into our idea of society is that it is not a way of inculcating collective responsibility so much as a way of letting everyone off the hook. If it's society's business, it's really nobody's business. Society appears here as a whole that has no individual parts. In *Strangers on a Train*, other people are not the synecdoche for society but the proof—in all their narrow self-interest and indifference—that the collective we lazily think of as a society doesn't actually include us, or any real person, at all.

Guy's epiphany about the nonexistence of society alters his own sense of personal responsibility. This is because responsibility makes no sense without recourse to a larger set of social norms:

> Did he care about rules? Wasn't it a rule that had kept him tied to Miriam? Wasn't it a person who was murdered, and therefore people who mattered? If people from Owen to Brillhart

> didn't care sufficiently to betray him, should he care any further? Why did he think this morning that he had wanted to give himself up to the police? What masochism was it? He wouldn't give himself up. What, concretely, did he have on his conscience now? What human being would inform on him?[35]

If there is no collective social body to care about what Guy has done, why should he care about it himself? In the absence of a society that abstractly governs the relations between individuals, guilt is nothing but "masochism": not an expression of social responsibility but—because there is no order that can be called social—a purely narcissistic form of self-punishment. Indeed, Highsmith suggests that the very idea of "conscience" is a social construct, in the strict sense that it, too, assumes the existence of society as a totalizing whole. What we think of as conscience is, in this passage, nothing but the unsustainable fantasy of a society that will hold one accountable for the actions one feels most guilty about. In a social world where no "human being would inform on" any other and where no one is willing to hold anyone else accountable, the issue is not simply that Guy's guilt doesn't matter. It is that, without the assumption of a larger society, it no longer counts as guilt at all.

Highsmith's antisocial riposte to social belonging—aimed at demystifying the fantasy of a society that could somehow exist above and beyond individually embodied interests—is itself the product of a historically specific kind of society. Terrified of the "enemy within" while working to undermine structures of social welfare and common belonging without, the anti-Communist, anti-Semitic, and homophobic culture of the early Cold War depended in a very real sense on the social regulation of interiority: on the rigorous policing of the gap between public sentiments and private desires, between what one was willing to say and what one really thought. At the most immediate level, *Strangers on a Train* registers its anxiety about this sort of policing through its fixation on privacy. As Guy puts it at the end of the novel, "My mistake was in telling a stranger my private business."[36] The emphasis on privacy marks *Strangers on a Train* as a distinctly Cold War crime novel, one preoccupied with the tension between private life and the public sphere.

In Highsmith's novel, this tension proves to be both threatened and threatening. While Guy understands the lesson of his criminal misadventures to be the mistake of disclosing his "private business," he is also extremely anxious about others' ability to keep their private thoughts to themselves. Other people's inaccessible thoughts are Guy's biggest worry; he is obsessed with his own inability to know what other people are thinking. Reflecting back on his relationship with his ex-fiancée Miriam, Guy thinks, "How sure he had once been that he possessed her, possessed her every frailest thought! Suddenly it seemed that all love was only a tantalizing, a horrible next-best to knowing! He knew not the smallest part of the new world in Miriam's mind now. Was it possible that the same thing could happen with Anne?"[37] The dynamic of patriarchal possession associated with heterosexual marriage is here extended as far as the mental realm: Guy once believed that he owned even Miriam's thoughts. But he was mistaken, and this mistake is indeed something that "could happen" and in fact will happen again and again. The inability to access the "world" of someone else's mind is the dilemma that defines Guy's entire world, not just with his ex-fiancée but also with his new fiancée, Anne: "She spoke slowly, and Guy was all at once terrified, realizing she was a separate person from himself, a person with a different mind."[38]

Of course, Guy's terror at realizing that he can't know his girlfriend's thoughts is largely a projection of his fear that she might know his—and, in knowing them, discover that the innocent person he claims to be on the outside isn't the guilty person he knows himself to be on the inside. In this way, crime turns out to be the name the novel gives to the mismatch between thought and expression, interiority and exteriority—an inner life of deviance versus an outer life of what the novel repeatedly calls "happiness." Everyone in the book wants everyone else to be happy, and everyone thinks everyone is happy except them. Happiness is what Guy's fiancée Anne has and Guy lacks; it is what Bruno never has except when he is with Guy; it is what Guy never feels with Bruno. "I know you have it in you, Guy," says Anne, "the capacity to be terribly happy."[39] Happiness, for Highsmith, is another name for social normativity. It is also the novel's measure of deviance. Guy is tormented not merely by his own unhappiness but by the awareness that his unhappiness makes him abnormal. Another way to put this is that it is really the self-conscious awareness of not being happy that makes Guy unhappy. Happiness in the novel is less a state of mind than it is the ideal of not having to deal with your own mind. And unhappiness, in turn, is simply the problem of thinking too much about happiness.

Or perhaps it is just the problem of thinking too much in general—the problem of having unconfessable thoughts. Guy is unhappy because his guilt over the murder of Bruno's murder can't be expressed. Bruno is unhappy because his sexual desire for Guy can't be admitted. What crime and queer desire have in common in Highsmith's novel—where they are explicitly conjoined—is that they both exemplify the ways that the social realm sustains itself by suppressing private thought. In Highsmith's view, the idea of society is the fantasy of a world in which the inner forms of guilt, anxiety, perversity, and desire don't exist, a world in which there is never any misalignment between what we think and what we say. But of course, that misalignment is always there, a fact we are reminded of by the very last line of *Strangers on a Train*: "Guy tried to speak, and said something entirely different from what he had intended. 'Take me.'"[40] The gap between speech and intention is also the gap between thought and word, a guilty conscience and a happy face. *Strangers on a Train* thus seeks to reassert the primacy of interiority against a repressive social order that convinces us it exists by pretending that the gap between a person's outward persona and inner thoughts doesn't. For Highsmith, it is because we live in a world in which *everyone* has secret thoughts, in which no one ever means what they say, that the idea of a society based on communication and consensus can only be an illusion.

Getting Away from Others

Crime rendered as a metaphor for society—or more specifically, as a metaphor for the impossibility of society—is even more vividly and viciously staged by the pulp writer Jim Thompson in his 1958 novel *The Getaway*. *The Getaway* tells the story of Doc and Carol McCoy, a husband-and-wife criminal team who rob a bank and end up on the run, killing many people along the way (including their partner in the robbery) before eventually escaping to Mexico with the heist money. Once there, they discover a new and unsettling kind of social order. This is the veritably antisocial order of the kingdom of El Rey, who offers refuge to criminals on the lam. But living in El Rey's kingdom comes with a catch: the cost. "All accommodations—everything one must buy—are strictly first class," and in this way, the kingdom is meticulously designed to slowly and inevitably drain the savings of the criminals who flock there.[41] If you don't put your money in El Rey's bank, it will likely be stolen, but if you do put it there, it is you who will have to pay interest to the bank for holding it:

> On balances of one hundred thousand dollars or more, the rate is six percent; but on lesser sums it rises, sharply, reaching a murderous twenty-five percent on amounts of fifty thousand and under. Briefly, it is almost imperative that a patron keep his account at or above the one hundred thousand figure. But he may not do this by a program of skimping and doing without. When one's monthly withdrawals fall under an arbitrary cost—the approximate amount which it should cost him to live at the prevailing first-class scale—he becomes subject to certain "inactive account" charges. And these, added to his withdrawals, invariably equal that total.[42]

Thus do the citizens of El Rey have no choice but to watch "their assets trickle, nay, pour away on every side."[43]

What happens when those assets run out, as they are designed to do? Doc discovers the answer when, one day, he takes a stroll into the neighboring village, whose "one street was attractively cobblestoned" and whose air was filled with the enticing "smell of roasting peppery meat."[44] The village turns out to be a "cooperative" in which "each resident contributes such labor as he is able to."[45] Weary of the rapacious capitalist conditions of El Rey and perhaps seduced by the echoes of Marx, Doc is enchanted by the idea of moving to the cooperative—that is, until he is told that there is "no drink or food of any kind" for sale in the village. What do the people there eat, then? The answer, Doc discovers, is present in the "*smell that filled the air. The odor of peppery, roasting flesh.*

Peppers could be had anywhere, for the picking, the asking, but the meat . . ." That's right: the residents of the village, sent there from El Rey when their savings are finally depleted, survive by cooking and eating each other. As Doc's guide to the village puts it to him, "Quite fitting, eh, *señor*? And such an easy transition. One need only live literally as he has always done figuratively."[46] What seems at first like an opposition between the mercenary economy of El Rey and the cooperative structure of the village is, on second look, a mirror. In the shadow of capitalism, "cooperation" is simply another word for cannibalism—and cannibalism, in turn, simply the truth of a capitalist order organized by nothing but self-interest in the service of self-preservation.

The kingdom of El Rey thus stands as an ornate allegory for the dissipation of cooperative social relations in capitalist society. Indeed, as Thompson's narrator tells us, in El Rey, "there is almost no social life." Trapped in a place where a person's sole concern is making his savings last as long as possible, people have neither need for nor interest in each other, and so "anyone approaching another is suspect or suspicious."[47] As for the kingdom itself, it is the spitting image of the laissez-faire, noninterventionist state. Here every criminal is left to their own vices and devices; El Rey "will not cheat you. He will not kill you. He cannot and will not provide for you, but he will not put an end to your life, no matter how long you live."[48] This is the paragon of a liberal society detached from any notion of the social whole or social good, a world where neither your neighbors nor your government will "provide for you . . . no matter how long you live."

"The tiny area where El Rey is uncrowned king appears on no maps," Thompson informs us.[49] This is surely because, in Thompson's view, it is something like the map itself, a representation of the entirety of a U.S. society that had clearly become, in the two decades since Thompson had been employed by the WPA during the New Deal, decisively postwelfare. Just as the cooperative village represents both the literalization and the culmination of the principles that shape El Rey, so does El Rey—ostensibly opposed to and located outside the United States—literalize and distill the essential values of postwar America.

The value of these antisocial values is reiterated throughout

The Getaway. Doc's is a world in which social charm is a screen for criminal self-interest. On one hand, Doc is charming, amiable, sociable; he "was born popular; into a world where he was instantly liked and constantly reassured of his welcome. Everyone smiled, everyone was friendly, everyone was anxious to please him."[50] On the other hand, behind the superficiality of charm—behind the fact that Doc "liked to be liked"[51]—lies a deeper commitment to the values Doc first learned from his father: "that a man's best friend is himself, that a non-friend was anyone who ceased to be useful, and that it was more or less a moral obligation to cash in any persons in this category, whenever it could be done safely and with no chance of a kickback."[52] The imperative to "cash in" persons the moment they no longer serve a use represents a kind of "moral obligation" that does not resemble morality much at all. This way of viewing other people as momentarily useful and ultimately disposable culminates in the cannibalism of the cooperative village, but it is present in the novel well before. In fact, it is even the secret to Doc and Carol's seemingly happy marriage: "she was his wife. . . . And if circumstances compelled him to think of her as an opponent—and he was not sure that they did, just yet—it was with no less love and a very great deal of regret."[53] For Doc, the distinction between "wife" and "opponent" is finally immaterial. After all, "as a professional criminal, he had schooled himself against placing complete trust in anyone."[54] In this way, Thompson uses the married criminals of *The Getaway* as the master symbols of a society in which social bonds have disintegrated, and where the best we can aspire to in our relations with others is to be as thin as thieves.

Outsider Art

The link between criminality, society, and literary form similarly preoccupied Richard Wright. Wright's 1953 opus *The Outsider* tells the story of Cross Damon, a Black postal worker living in Chicago who longs to escape the stifling constraints of his social obligations to his children, his wife, his mistress, and his mother: "He had to break with others and, in breaking with them, he would break with himself. He must sever all ties of memory and sentimentality."[55] He is given the chance at precisely such a break when he is involved in a train crash and the body of another Black passenger is mistaken for his own. Presumed dead, Cross leaves Chicago for New York to live out the radical freedom of his new identity—a freedom that consists primarily in having lengthy arguments with members of the Communist Party and, later on, in murdering several of them.

Wright wrote *The Outsider* while in exile in France and under the strong influence of existentialism, and he hoped that the novel's publication would allow African American literature to escape the shadow that was still cast by his own 1940 classic of social protest, *Native Son*. Yet, Wright predicted to his friend and protégé Ralph Ellison about *The Outsider*, "Negroes will not like it."[56] The reason, Wright assumed, was because the story of Cross Damon was at heart a story about rejecting all forms of social determination, obligation, and identification—including those of race. As Wright's narrator says of Cross, "being a Negro was the least important thing in his life."[57] Though to be fair, plenty of other things have no importance to Cross: his embrace of radical freedom means rejecting the ties—of race, community, family, and political affiliation—that, in his mind, make society less a fabric than a fabrication. All it takes to give the lie to society and social obligation, Cross realizes, is simply no longer to feel obligated to it. He embodies just the act and the fact of refusing to associate:

> At some point in his past life . . . he had come to a consciousness of having somehow fallen into a vast web of pledges and promises which he had not intended to make and whose implied obligations had been slowly smothering his spirit; and, by a stroke of freakish good luck [i.e., the train accident], he had been able to rip the viscous strands of that web and fling them behind him. . . . He knew, of course, that his commitments were no more galling or burdensome than those which other millions of men and women about him shouldered so uncomplainingly every day; yet he knew that deep in the hearts of many of those millions was the same desire—shamefaced, inarticulate, and impotent—to have done with them as he had.[58]

Wright thus used the character of Cross Damon as a kind of thought experiment, a test of what it would look like to extricate oneself fully from the "web of pledges and promises" that forges social belonging and social identity through the ingrained rituals of social obligation. Wright's gambit is that the potential value of this thought experiment is not confined to Cross alone; "deep in the hearts" of "millions of men and women," he imagines, is "the same desire" Cross has to escape one's social commitments. At the heart of what makes up society, in other words, is the "shamefaced, inarticulate" truth of antisocial sentiment.

The pinnacle of such sentiment is what the novel calls "ethical murder," by which Wright means not so much killing for good reason as killing for no reason whatsoever. "These killings will be marked unsolved," Cross's nemesis, the district attorney Eli Houston, tells him. "And, in a sense, they are. Even now I cannot say why you killed in a rational manner."[59] The withholding of any motive for his killing is Cross's most disturbing antisocial feat. "Oh, God in Heaven! Why *did* you kill him?" Cross's love interest, Eva, asks him. "'I don't know,' he whispered. '*Why*? There must be some *reason* . . .' He shook his head. . . . 'I don't *believe* in anything.'"[60] This lack of belief in any kind of social responsibility or prohibition is what links Cross's repudiation of social bonds to his acts of motiveless murder. It is also what eventually allows Houston, the DA, to solve the crimes:

> At first I didn't believe it, but when you stared so unfeelingly at your sons, when you laughed when your poor wife could not summon enough strength to identify you, I knew that you were beyond the pale of all the *little* feelings, the *humble* feelings, the *human* feelings . . . *I knew that you could do anything*! Not in a towering rage, not to save falling mankind, not to establish social justice, not for glory. . . . But just because you happen to feel like that one day.[61]

The final explanation for how Cross could murder without reason is to be found in his refusal of the most basic social "feelings," which are here synonymous with basic social obligations. The person who acknowledges no social connections whatsoever is the person who is capable of doing anything, for the simple reason that he has no reason not to do it.

But what in the first place enables Cross's "contemptuous repudiation of all the fundamental promises that men live by"?[62] It is his sense that those promises—the commitments among people that constitute a social order—have, in the modern societies of the industrialized West, already decayed beyond recognition. As Cross sees them, the "great cities of the earth today—Chicago, Detroit, Pittsburg, London, Manchester, Paris, Tokyo, Hong Kong," are now only "vast pools of human misery, networks of raw human nerves exposed without benefit of illusion or hope to the new, godless world wrought by industrial man. Industrial life plus a rampant capitalism have blasted the lives of men in these cities. . . . The people of these cities are lost."[63] The degraded social conditions of urban modernity are thus the precondition for Cross's social repudiation. To live among the lost souls of the West's urban centers is finally to be, as Cross is, only "vaguely conscious of other people whose presence seemed remote and unimportant."[64] At the core both of Cross's murders and of his repudiation of his social and familial obligations is, finally, this elemental truth of modern urban life: the remoteness and ultimate insignificance of "other people."

The Antisocial Order

Read together, *The Outsider*, *The Getaway*, and *Strangers on a Train* exemplify a cultural moment defined by radical skepticism about the nature of social obligation and the possibility of social relations. Wright's antisocial antihero has "cynically scorned, wantonly violated every commitment that civilized men owe."[65] Thompson's affable criminal escapes to a place where "there is almost no social life." Highsmith's anxious architect is no longer certain it is "people who mattered." What, finally, was the point for these authors of writing fiction that so perfectly matched the sentiments of their antisocial era?

At the time, the loss of conviction that other people mattered grew, in part, out of a growing skepticism that other people could be known or understood at all. Friedrich Hayek, one of the founding fathers of microeconomics, put it this way in 1948: "It is not only impossible to recognize, but meaningless to speak of, a mind different from our own."[66] The impossibility of knowing other minds was a pressing issue for Wright, Thompson, and Highsmith. We've already seen how this works in *Strangers on a Train*, where Guy is wracked with worry about the inaccessible secrets lodged in other people's minds: "Guy was all at once terrified, realizing she was . . . a person with a different mind." Guy is not alone in his terror of other people's irreducible unknowability. In *The Getaway*, Doc's perpetually affable demeanor becomes a source of deep dread for his wife, Carol: "He could be breaking apart inside and you'd never know it from the way he acted. He'd be just as pleasant and polite as if he didn't have a care in the world. You had to be careful with someone like that. You could never know what he was thinking."[67] If you can "never know [. . .] from the way he acted" what someone actually thinks, then you can no longer believe in the possibility of a social world that is legitimately shared.[68] This is the disturbing possibility that Cross confronts directly at the end of *The Outsider*: "Was there really no direct bridge between the subjective worlds of people? Was the possibility of communication only a kind of pretense, an arrangement assumed to exist but which really did not?"[69] The "pretense" Cross has in mind here is nothing less than the pretense of society—the fantasy that so many impenetrable "subjective worlds" can really be assumed to come together to form some sort of social whole.

Is there any way to solve this problem, any means to "bridge" the seemingly separate "subjective worlds of people"? In response to this question, all three novelists suggest that the novel form itself might contain an answer. That answer is connected to the novel's special capacity to render private thought in a publicly shared, quasi-objective form. The technical name for this capacity is free indirect discourse, and it is the defining literary style of all three novels I have been discussing. It is therefore not quite right to imply, as I did in the preceding paragraph, that in *The Outsider*, it is Cross who wonders, "Was there really no direct bridge between the subjective worlds of people?" Because Wright fuses Cross's thought with third person narration, it is, in truth, not actually clear whose idea this is. It isn't exactly Cross's, and it isn't exactly not. "Were we really that much alone in this life?" Cross or the narrator asks a few lines later. "Was the core of the subjective life of each person sealed off absolutely from that of another and one could tell what transpired in another heart only when the contents of that heart were projected outwardly in some objective form?"[70] In fact, the isolation Cross feels is already interrupted by the impossibility of saying who has said this. If the depth of his "subjective life" is what kept Cross "sealed off" from other people, what he needs to break the seal and rediscover sociality is the outward projection of some "objective form" of his inner life. That objective form is nothing less than the form Wright has bestowed on his novel. This is the literary form of free indirect style, which does exactly what Cross deems necessary: it turns subjectivity into objectivity, isolation into connection, by transforming the "contents" of his heart and mind into the ostensibly "objective form" of omniscient narration.

Likewise, in *Strangers on a Train,* Highsmith's thematic commitment to the social crisis provoked by private thought is managed by a formal commitment to free indirect discourse—a literary style uniquely capable of giving us access to all those secret, guilty thoughts that might otherwise give the lie to social belonging. At several points, Highsmith goes to extreme lengths to make clear just how expansively the style operates in her novel. Take this short passage: "She looked increasingly loathsome, so he began not to want to put his hands on her soft sticky-warm flesh. Well, he still had the knife. A clean instrument. 'A clean instrument!' Bruno shouted jubilantly, for no one could possibly hear him."[71] It is unusual to find a line of unattributed narration repeated verbatim as dialogue. What is Highsmith up to here? The repetition of the line "A clean instrument" at once confirms and inflames our suspicion that everything a reader has assumed to be omniscient narration might really be subjective thought. Put more starkly, the repetition suggests that, in *Strangers on a Train,* such a distinction may finally be immaterial. If privacy is what Guy prizes in himself and fears in others, it is what the novel itself renders meaningless.

Actually, it is what *every* novel renders meaningless. There is no such thing as privacy in fiction, and no such thing as private thought in the literature of free indirect style, which not only exposes the hidden thoughts of its characters but transforms those thoughts into the building blocks of the novel's objective language.[72] This is equally the case in *The Getaway*, where Carol's implicitly first person anxieties about Doc's implacable demeanor—*I*, she implies, "could never know what he was thinking"—are translated, by way of the royal "you," into a universally applicable social rule: "you had to be careful with someone like that." In the sociopathic novels of Wright, Highsmith, and Thompson, free indirect discourse represents the "objective form" that makes private being indistinguishable from public expression, that turns inner life into social life.

In short, these novels think through what it would look like for it to *not* be (pace Hayek) "meaningless to speak of a mind different from our own." The content of other minds conveyed through free indirect discourse—the X-ray vision of this quintessentially modern type of novelistic narration—is ultimately a way of communicating the possibility of social or collective life as such. As Thompson puts it in *The Getaway*, "You cannot do what you must unaided."[73] Cross learns the very same lesson at the end of *The Outsider*: "The search can't be done alone."[74] The necessity of aid, the overcoming of solitude: these turn out to be the unexpected truths of the antisocial novel written in an antisocial age.

This conclusion is not without some irony. After all, both Doc and Cross are doomed to learn such lessons much too late: Cross on his deathbed, McCoy on the verge of becoming food for his fellow thieves. Moreover, such a conclusion risks banalizing the antisocial novel and misunderstanding its social function, which is not so much to ask, *should people work together and aid one another?* (surely they should) as it is to wonder, *why don't they?*

On this point, all three novels provide a more counterintuitive answer. In the antisocial actions of Doc McCoy, Guy Haines, and Cross Damon, what we find is not evidence that society doesn't exist. What we find is evidence that it does. Literary antisociality in 1950s crime fiction was not only the mirror of an era's waning belief in social collectivity. It was also the historically specific product of that era's particular forms of not only of social organization but also of social exclusion. For Thompson, Doc's antisocial commitment to nothing but his own self-interest is the product of a capitalist system that had just recently begun to systematically abandon its most vulnerable workers, such as the sharecroppers Doc meets, who are so impoverished and cut off from liberal society that they were essentially "an autonomous body, functioning within a society which was organized to grind them down."[75] For Highsmith, Guy's and Bruno's shared belief in the inviolability of private thought is ultimately a reflection of a homophobic society that polices certain forms of private sexual desire; this is why Bruno's suppressed criminal impulses are ultimately indistinguishable from his repressed queer desire: "Everything was silly compared to the night in Metcalf. Every person he knew was silly compared to Guy. Silliest of all to think he'd wanted to see a lot of European women!"[76] For Wright, finally, even Cross's self-styled stance as a social outsider is merely a literalization of the forms of de jure and de facto segregation that shaped American society at midcentury: "In America the Negro is outside. Our laws and practices see to it that he stays outside."[77] To be Black in segregated America was to be part of a class of "men who had been rejected and yet who still lived and shared the lives of their rejectors."[78] This paradoxical stance—to be rejected while living among one's rejectors—is the most profound lesson imparted by the midcentury American novel's antisocial antiheroes.

Social withdrawal doesn't work unless there is something to withdraw from. And the way someone like Cross knows that there *is* a society to withdraw from is that he has been forced to live outside it. At the end of *The Outsider*, Cross is devastated to realize that he will not be held accountable for his crimes: "He had broken all of his promises to the world and the people in it, but he had never reckoned on that world turning on him and breaking its promise to him too! . . . Men would not give meaning to what he had done! Society would not even look at it, recognize it! That was not fair, wasn't right, just."[79] A character who earlier insisted on the illusory nature of social bonds now invokes the collective viewpoint of a "society" that will barely "look at" let alone "recognize" him. With these lines, which echo not only Guy's final regret at his own failed confession but also Carol's self-deluding request to be told that social connection really does make a difference ("T-tell me it does, Doc, and I'll tell you it does"[80]), the antisocial novel of the 1950s confirms that its aim is not so much to repudiate society as it is to investigate what it means to be repudiated *by* society—a concept whose abstract yet undeniable and above all unjust existence, it turns out, has been haunting these novels all along.

In the novels I've been discussing, the antisocial criminal act turns out to be less a gesture of radical freedom than a desperate attempt at social recognition. What these thrusts at recognition underscore are the resolutely social, rather than individual, processes of exploitation and exclusion that organize human life in capitalist modernity: the structuring antisocial imperatives of a market whose newfound "freedom" is made possible by the vigorous policing of race and sexuality.[81] Such imperatives were nothing less than the lived realities of postwar liberal society writ large, and the attention paid to them in these seemingly antisocial novels—one written by a closeted queer woman who wrote lesbian pulp fiction under a pseudonym, another by a Black man who grew up amid the racial violence of Jim Crow, and a third by a former Communist who directed the Oklahoma Federal Writers Project during the New Deal—is not hard to explain. For these writers, the politics of being antisocial are located not in the gesture of setting oneself outside society but in the grim apprehension of how society structures itself by setting certain groups of people outside it.

The unexpected invocation of the group in these novels—queer people in *Strangers on a Train*, African Americans in *The Outsider*, poor farm workers in *The Getaway*—may seem merely a symptomatic index of what scholars of postwar politics have disparagingly referred to as the era's "interest-group liberalism."[82] Yet the thing that defines a group in all three novels is not their shared interests. It is their ascriptive constitution and their socially exterior position. To live "on a racially defined edge of [. . .] society," Karen and Barbara Fields write in their book *Racecraft*, is "to experience the social intuitively as a realm fundamentally distinct from the realm of nature." This intuitive grasp of the social realm, this view of the social whole from outside it, is rooted in the irreducible social fact of "human groups—in the social and intellectual processes that designate groups, their boundaries, their members, and the place of all the foregoing in the larger cosmos."[83] In this way, the seemingly divisive or dispersive fiction of the group turns out to have a powerful heuristic function after all. Exposing the abstract social norms that invisibly yet inexorably structure all our ostensibly autonomous individual lives, the ascriptive group is at once the material evidence of society's antisocial origins and a stark rebuttal to the magic of antisocial thinking: a reminder of the very real ways our world is indeed shared, whether we like it or not.

Notes

1. David Alworth, *Site Reading: Fiction, Art, Social Form* (Princeton, N.J.: Princeton University Press, 2016), 4.
2. Bruno Latour, *Reassembling the Social: An Introduction to Actor-Network-Theory* (Oxford: Oxford University Press, 2005), 4.
3. Latour, 5.
4. On the roughly contemporaneous emergence of Latour's and Thatcher's theories of society's nonexistence, see Jodi Dean, "Society Doesn't Exist," *First Monday* 18, no. 3–4 (2013), https://doi.org/10.5210/fm.v18i3.4616.
5. Rita Felski, "Context Stinks!," *New Literary History* 42, no. 4 (2011): 578.
6. Émile Durkheim, *Selected Writings*, ed. and trans. Anthony Giddens (Cambridge: Cambridge University Press, 1972), 67.
7. Durkheim, 64, 66.
8. A different theoretical account of antisociality can be found in queer theory's "antisocial thesis." The antisocial thesis, most frequently associated with thinkers like Leo Bersani and Lee Edelman, emphasizes the negative potential of what Robert L. Caserio calls "queer unbelonging" as a site for questioning the liberal-capitalist norms of sociality, community, and (in Bersani's words) "civic service." Robert L. Caserio, "The Antisocial Thesis in Queer Theory," *PMLA* 121, no. 3 (2006): 819.
9. On the role of the novel in shoring up the "invisible community" of the nation-state, see Benedict Anderson, *Imagined Communities: Reflections on the Origin and Spread of Nationalism* (London: Verso, 1983); on the relation between the novel and the rise of consumer credit, see Deidre Shauna Lynch, *The Economy of Character: Novels, Market Culture, and the Business of Inner Meaning* (Chicago: University of Chicago Press, 1998).
10. On the centrality of "private experience" to the development of the novel, see Ian Watt, *The Rise of the Novel: Studies in Defoe, Richardson, and Fielding* (Berkeley: University of California Press, 1957),

esp. 174–207; on the novel's role in inventing the category of the modern individual, see Nancy Armstrong, *How Novels Think: The Limits of Individualism from 1719–1900* (New York: Columbia University Press, 2005).

11. "Among the novel's modern functions . . . was as a socially acceptable means of remaining detached while in public," writes Gage McWeeny. McWeeny, *The Comfort of Strangers: Social Life and Literary Form* (Oxford: Oxford University Press, 2016), 2.

12. On the historical emergence of the category of fiction, see Catherine Gallagher, "The Rise of Fictionality," in *The Novel, Vol. 1, History, Geography, and Culture*, ed. Franco Moretti, 336–363 (Princeton, N.J.: Princeton University Press, 2007); on fiction's defining capacity to mark "a strategic difference from reality," see Ian Duncan, *Scott's Shadow: The Novel in Romantic Edinburgh* (Princeton, N.J.: Princeton University Press, 2007), 29.

13. D. A. Miller, *The Novel and the Police* (Berkeley: University of California Press, 1988), 2.

14. Jeff Nunokawa, "Eros and Isolation: The Antisocial George Eliot," *ELH* 69, no. 4 (2002): 839.

15. Christopher Lane, *Hatred and Civility: The Antisocial Life in Victorian England* (New York: Columbia University Press, 2004), xvii.

16. Lane, 32.

17. McWeeny, *Comfort of Strangers*, 7, 25, 8.

18. For an indispensable account of how an earlier generation of American modernists was influenced by the social imaginary of the New Deal, in particular by its founding concept of social security, see Michael Szalay, *New Deal Modernism: American Literature and the Invention of the Welfare State* (Durham, N.C.: Duke University Press, 2000).

19. Ira Katznelson, "Was the Great Society a Lost Opportunity?," in *The Rise and Fall of the New Deal Order, 1930–1980*, ed. Steve Fraser and Gary Gerstle (Princeton, N.J.: Princeton University Press, 1989), 189.

20. On the far-reaching ideological implications of the teenage rebel, see Leerom Medovoi, *Rebels: Youth and the Cold War Origins of Identity* (Durham, N.C.: Duke University Press, 2005).

21. Katznelson, "Was the Great Society a Missed Opportunity?," 187.

22. Both the working-class gains of the New Deal and the middle-class prosperity of the 1950s were built on the exclusion of African Americans—a point to which I will return at the end of this essay. See Ira Katznelson, *When Affirmative Action Was White: An Untold*

History of Racial Inequality in Twentieth-Century America (New York: W. W. Norton, 2005).

23. Carol A. Horton, *Race and the Making of American Liberalism* (Oxford: Oxford University Press, 2005), 130.

24. Alan Brinkley, "The New Deal and the Idea of the State," in Fraser and Gerstle, *Rise and Fall of the New Deal Order, 1930–1980*, 101–2.

25. Horton, *Race and the Making of American Liberalism*, 128, 130.

26. Theodore J. Lowi, *The End of Liberalism: Ideology, Policy, and the Crisis of Public Authority* (New York: W. W. Norton, 1969), 48.

27. Katznelson, "Was the Great Society a Missed Opportunity?," 191.

28. Annie McClanahan, "Methodological Individualism and the Novel in the Age of Microeconomics, 1871 to the Present," in *Timelines of American Literature*, ed. Cody Marrs and Christopher Hager (Baltimore: Johns Hopkins University Press, 2019), 270, 271.

29. Sean McCann, *Gumshoe America: Hard-Boiled Crime Fiction and the Rise and Fall of New Deal Liberalism* (Durham, N.C.: Duke University Press, 2000), 199.

30. Leonard Cassuto, *Hard-Boiled Sentimentality: The Secret History of American Crime Stories* (New York: Columbia University Press, 2009), 125, 126.

31. Jean Comaroff and John L. Comaroff, *The Truth about Crime: Sovereignty, Knowledge, Social Order* (Chicago: University of Chicago Press, 2016), xiv.

32. Erving Goffman, *Stigma: Notes on the Management of Spoiled Identity* (New York: Simon and Schuster, 1963), 144.

33. Patricia Highsmith, *Strangers on a Train* (New York: W. W. Norton, 1993), 277.

34. Highsmith.

35. Highsmith, 278.

36. Highsmith, 271.

37. Highsmith, 38.

38. Highsmith, 162.

39. Highsmith, 54.

40. Highsmith, 281.

41. Jim Thompson, *The Getaway* (New York: Vintage Crime, 1994), 170.

42. Thompson, 171.

43. Thompson, 170.

44. Thompson, 173.

45. Thompson, 174.

46. Thompson, 175.

47. Thompson, 173.

48. Thompson, 178.
49. Thompson, 169.
50. Thompson, 25.
51. Thompson, 127.
52. Thompson, 43.
53. Thompson, 168.
54. Thompson, 71.
55. Richard Wright, *The Outsider,* restored text (New York: Harper Perennial, 1991), 114.
56. Quoted in Paula Rabinowitz, *Black and White and Noir: America's Pulp Modernism* (New York: Columbia University Press, 2002), 87.
57. Wright, *Outsider,* 385.
58. Wright, 503.
59. Wright, 572.
60. Wright, 531.
61. Wright, 564.
62. Wright, 501.
63. Wright, 485.
64. Wright, 582.
65. Wright, 501.
66. Quoted in McClanahan, "Methodological Individualism and the Novel," 270.
67. Thompson, *Getaway,* 148.
68. Michael Trask argues that a certain kind of performativity—and the fluid identities and identifications implied therein—was a core feature of Cold War liberalism. Liberalism, in Trask's account, was above all about the performance of beliefs and commitments one wasn't actually expected to believe in or remain committed to: "In the postwar ideal of social order, persons were compelled by no regulatory agency more onerous than their agreement to behave as if an institution had a constraining effect on their actions that no one honored except in the breach." Trask, *Camp Sites: Sex, Politics, and Academic Style in Postwar America* (Stanford, Calif.: Stanford University Press, 2013), 3.
69. Wright, *Outsider,* 446.
70. Wright.
71. Highsmith, *Strangers on a Train,* 78.
72. Theorists of the realist novel have long noted the fact that the form depends on a kind of invasion of privacy, an entry into the private space of the home. As Peter Brooks explains, the realist novel is premised on the act of "seeing through the roofs . . . to the private

lives behind and beneath." In *The Rise of the Novel,* Watt offers an even more evocative metaphor: "the novelist in the house of fiction is, if not that of the peeper through the keyholes, at least that of the 'watcher at the window'" (200). Brooks, *Realist Vision* (New Haven, Conn.: Yale University Press, 2005), 3.

73. Thompson, *Getaway,* 122.

74. Wright, *Outsider,* 585.

75. Thompson, *Getaway,* 123.

76. Highsmith, *Strangers on a Train,* 218.

77. Wright, *Outsider,* 170.

78. Wright, 111. For more on the racialized character of literary criminality in the 1950s, see my "Crime Fiction and Black Criminality," *American Literary History* 30, no. 4 (2018): 703–29.

79. Wright, 573.

80. Thompson, *Getaway,* 184.

81. On the "unique structure of state violence and social emancipation" that has defined U.S. liberalism throughout the twentieth and twenty-first centuries, see Chandan Reddy, *Freedom with Violence: Race, Sexuality, and the U.S. State* (Durham, N.C.: Duke University Press, 2011), 37.

82. Lowi famously defined the "new American public philosophy" that emerged after World War II as interest-group liberalism. Lowi, *End of Liberalism,* 71. This brand of liberalism emerged out of a pluralist worldview that, pitting itself against Marxism, understood power not as divided between two classes but as widely "dispersed" among groups: "Groups, of which corporations are merely one type, possess power directly over a segment of society and also a share of control of the state." The major consequence of this view of the group as the "dominant reality of modern life" was to render things like universal struggle or unified class interest impossible: "As long as even a small proportion of all interests remains strong and active, no unitary political class, or 'power elite,' will emerge. That is, in the pluralist system it is highly improbable that a consensus across a whole class can last long enough to institutionalize itself" (45). Thus, as Sean McCann explains in *Gumshoe America,* following Lowi, "to be a democratic subject" in the postwar United States "did not entail a direct role in self-government; nor did it make one a faceless member of a mass constituency. It meant, rather, that one belonged to one or more of the various 'support group constituencies' that negotiated through the state over the direction of society" (34–35). The idea of a society con-

tingently hammered out through the negotiations of competing groups radically transformed the liberal theory of the state. As Lowi elaborated in *The End of Liberalism*, "the zeal of pluralism for the group and its belief in a natural harmony of group competition tended to break down the very ethic of government by reducing the essential conception of government to nothing more than another set of mere interest groups" (48). In a political system shaped by interest-group liberalism, "the role of government is one of ensuring access particularly to the most effectively organized [groups], and of ratifying the agreements and adjustments worked out among the competing leaders and their claims" (71). As a result, the battle between liberalism and conservatism was no longer a battle over competing definitions of the function of the state. Instead, Lowi concluded, "*the most important difference between liberals and conservatives, Republicans and Democrats . . . is to be found in the interest groups they identify with*" (72, emphasis original).

83. Karen E. Fields and Barbara J. Fields, *Racecraft: The Soul of Inequality in American Life* (London: Verso, 2012), 237, 260.

3

The Big and Small No

Critique of Contemporary Solutions of Difference (Deleuze and Derrida)

François Laruelle

Translated by Anthony Paul Smith

To construct a new ascending and descending dialectic, we will use a more complex operation than the No. It is the combination of the "Without," or the French *sans*, and the No and Yes relative to each other and in a way that is processual rather than static. They are taken from two contemporary, and so post-Hegelian, philosophers: Derrida and Deleuze. Against the solitude of their interjection, the No and the Yes must be coupled into a dyad construction that puts them in motion and that has always been called philosophy, or the dialectic. These interjections, an interdiction and an affirmation, are assumed to be autoreferents and absolute, without any possible discussion, and this is a way of not thinking, of refusing thought. A "flawless" prohibition.

This more complex, two-winged operator—which is the relative "without" and which puts thought in motion, combines the relative negation and/for a revival of affirmation, but one that will not be reduced to a simple correlation or coupling—this operator is a process. The medium of these two gestures must be the same to be fruitful, and therefore complex as well, to be able to support not only a subtraction that is still insufficient although necessary to get a multiplication under way. This is not an interjection or prohibition addressed to ——, it is a productive "without" or one of amplification working under a given that is itself complex. There is something here of the imperative or performative gesture, but always remaining as an action of amplification when it would only be meaning, blood, and so on.

Therefore this is not exactly Derrida's "blood of the pure cut" that here seems to privilege the cut and subtraction but emends in a second moment the affirmative flow of blood, of the smear, the affirmative nature of difference, so coming back to Nietzsche, in fact, a Nietzsche quite weakened because the important thing for Derrida is the cut or Judaic "cutting off" [*retranchement*], not really the Deleuzian reaffirmation of Nietzsche. It is true that Deleuze retroactively assumed affirmation under the form of the active force that Derrida did not take on, instead taking on logocentrism, which in its way is a first affirmation but one that would have to begin through a reversal or cutting off. Just as in Deleuze, there is an initial or active reversal of reactive inversion as a point of departure into deficiency that is also "logocentric," but technically less utilized than in Derrida's work, for whom the reversal is apparently inaugural and essential, more than the affirmation as reaffirmation for Deleuze, and which is worth a second gesture. Deleuze is more Nietzschean, Derrida is more Judaic, indeed, everyone already knows this; still it is necessary to pay attention to the respective weights of these two contrary gestures and everything each presents. For Derrida, the cutting off is the most important thing or is worth more than sticking things back together or the final synthesis, which remains weak; for Deleuze, it is the reaffirmation or amplified synthesis. Indeed, one of their distinctions is not between active and reactive forces—there is a superior distinction between an affirmative and negative will to power. In other words, Derrida makes do with difference as withdrawal or "retreat" and cutting off or "recutting," and he adds to it affirmation or the flow of blood by way of amplification, while Deleuze overcomes and surpasses the a priori through the transcendental, which does not mean that Derrida ignores the transcendental but to deconstruct it and its power of One. Judaism forbids him the most speculative logos; certainly Derrida does not ignore it but quickly deconstructs it. Derrida privileges the "no" without ignoring every affirmation, but he ignores the affirmative "yes" as reaffirmative. The antinomy of Deleuze and Derrida remains an antinomy within the limits of philosophy as a Principle of Philosophical Sufficiency (PPS); this is why they are opposed on the usage of it—they are divided between a redoubled No and a redoubled Yes because they remain within the transcendental, the one to deconstruct it and the other to affirm it. This is the surest sign that they remain within the PPS, where they lock themselves up as lovers who share the same bed or the same conjugality. But an operation must be closed on itself or be made into a circle of addition. So does it assume a set object that is not evasive even though relative-absolute? It is a relation with the radical as a return to the root and a starting again from it that can be open and evasive. The radical seems to be a stage within the circle of the absolute, which is firmer. Both recognize the duality of this tempered dialectic but throw it off balance and, above all, balance it in a different way, through an aggravation or a supplement of weight placed on withdrawal or even affirmation as, for example, reaffirmation that Derrida does not realize.

Each of these gestures must be aggravated, the withdrawal of theological essence and more, for the one, and the will to power as reaffirmation, for the other. Their difference begins with the generic either as cut or as subtraction of −1, either Judaic or algebraic, and continues with the affirmation of blood that flows either as reaffirmation of the philosophical circle as eternal return of the same or as an effusion of a wound, so according to two very different models.

With a mind to prepare for our own problematic of Reminscience and to tear it away from spontaneous philosophy as received from the tradition, we will retain from the preceding scene (in order to transform it, of course) two essential traits. One, the generic of the Deleuzian withdrawal as mathematics, but which we will put forward within the limits of human experience which prepares access to philosophy properly so called but which is not yet it, or just its worldly preparation. And two, the quasi-religious atmosphere of the inscription of this gesture put into the Nietzschean account and so still ambiguous because theological, regarding God and the Universe, and again, we must choose what is the most fecund meaning of the Universe for us. On the whole we will choose Deleuze for his philosophico-physical choice rather than Derrida for his theologico-linguistic choice, meaning "writing" in every sense of the term.

However, in this choice, which remains a prisoner to the primacy of philosophy, Deleuze is for us still insufficient because it is not thermodynamics that is the most effective scientific reference for the establishment of Reminscience, even if Deleuze's choices are necessary for a critique of psychoanalysis. If all these syntactical descriptions are excellent, it is necessary to change the ground they are on, to transplant them onto the quantum and as a result to transplant also withdrawal onto the terrain of "light" mathematical experience, as Deleuze did indeed do. But if there is a supplementary step to implement, it is fundamentally that of the quantum or of the Universe wrenched away from the Greek mythology of the Eternal Return of the Same (ERS) and away from its basis in still-Newtonian thermodynamics. This tearing away for "another" Universe leads to that of the generic, which allows for human genericity to be thought scientifically and not religiously. It is a digging up of this syntax and its reimplantation onto a new terrain that is itself double.

The supplementary step beyond Deleuze is that of the passage to the plane of generic-quantum Reminscience. We are transitioning little by little toward a certain Kantian and even Marxian dualism to give meaning to this double transplantation, because the problem is not one of sticking together, to separate the generic and the philosophical even if they have similar syntaxes, not to try to identify them too simply within a single ascendant dialectic, as Badiou has done; otherwise, the science invoked is too strong in the face of philosophy, which nevertheless aspires to or absorbs it finally. The duality of the strata allows a double or divided and inverted dialectic and not an immobile or rigid structure. For ourselves, we carry out a double turn in relation to our first attempts, a new concept of the Universe, from ERS with its Greek essence to the quantum Universe, and from the a priori of experience to the genericity of it, so a movement toward more mathematical rigor, here introduced, but not toward a total-mathematics, as Badiou does, for example. It is also a return to physics against total-mathematics, a modification of the terrain of implantation which passes from philosophy and/or from the mythology that abandons its too-excessive mathematicism, to a scientific form of experience and a general elevation of instances in this way reinforced by their passage to non-philosophy and nonstandard philosophy. In this way, we re-traverse our entire trajectory, from Nietzsche or from Deleuze to Derrida to the philosophico-musical synthesis.

It is also a complete reorganization of the topology of thought, because the transcendental or the philosophical, which remains our major instrument, is transformed and displaced with regard to its fundamental role toward a status that is auxiliary to the fundamental that is based in the quantum. The foundation is thus shared between a base and governance, between the carrier boat and the rudder which sets its direction, the two attached or functioning synergistically; the boat which is not attached to human experience as a "transcendental generic" replaces the "aesthetic" by virtue of its overdetermination by and within the Universe.

Within contemporary philosophy there is a conflict or an antinomy of the No and the Yes, a typically philosophical antinomy that we must overcome by placing it again within the broader context we call the "Reminsc-I-ence." This conflict is never absolute in its terms, and consequentially, it is never absolute as such. Absolute terms would not be able to enter into the order of philosophical discussion but strictly into the moral, as a prohibition for the No and within religion or within an amorous relation of adoration for the Yes. In both cases, it is a nondiscourse, a nonlogos, a No of prohibition without discussion or of refusal without concession, or a Yes of consent here also without discussion or reserve.

But philosophy cannot be, save for an explicit contract that seems to exclude it, an absolute demand for prohibition or even obedience; at any rate, it assumes linguistic mediation rather than the obedience or performativity of the plea. It would otherwise be a situation of conflict rather than of dialogic, which always leads to hoping for a final peaceful resolution to the brutality of the antinomy, even if it must pass through tactics or, indeed, strategy. In other words, a certain negotiation is inevitable, except the annihilation of one term by the other—this annihilation may be on the order of obedience or adoration and fusion. The philosophers have accepted a final resolution to this kind of conflict; I dare say that it is their "good sense" (Kant and Hegel through a rational resolution of the antinomies of the understanding, Kierkegaard through faith, and even Heidegger through "co-propriation" or the "mutual belonging" [*Zussammengehörigkeit*] of Dasein to Being), not to mention at another level psychoanalysis. A solution is possible by virtue of the relativity of the No to the Yes, the one for the other and so of a superior circle in which they are enclosed, and therefore by their very overcoming or their transcendence toward their relative-absolute unity. The antinomy finally demands the transcendental dimension under any form whatsoever. Hence the passage from the big No of Mephistophelean refusal to the philosophical and dispersible No, and then to the big Yes of Nietzschean reaffirmation. Both are certainly animated by a will to autoposition or autoreference, either at first or finally, but must be composed dialectically with the complexity of the real.

In all of this the radical has escaped us, Descartes and Husserl; the radical finds its fusion with the absolute, but it is not the absolute or only it through its effect and its gains. At best, as a return to the root and a recasting toward the absolute (the veracious God, absolutely grounded knowledge), it, too, is immediately caught in a circle and ends up in another circle heading in the opposite direction, but it is more honest than the absolute No and the absolute Yes since it reveals the basic mechanism necessary for every complex movement of this kind. Derrida had the merit of instilling in the philosophers an understanding (certainly not the discovery) of this dialectic internal to negation and affirmation in the guise, for example, of the "blood of the pure cut," meaning the a priori, which by himself he could not escape from this wound which has just been made, and which is the affirmation (though certainly very weak) of new life. It is here that one sees a new antinomy appear within this contemporary philosophy that is so educated, well informed, scholarly, and careful. The radical refers to the ground of the foundation from which one must leave or begin, or return. Let us therefore leave the radical, leave the root as a function of the Cartesian tree: it is definitely an obsession of Descartes, the tree after the forest, one not hiding the other and even in reality cooperating as two always-expected opposites. We begin with a very general antinomy in order to begin to examine the position of this problem in two contemporary philosophers.

So what within this dialectic can specify the radical and distinguish it from the absolute? The radical is the first gesture and so the default or abasement, the symbol of lack or withdrawal. The absolute is the second and final reconciliation and mutual belonging. It is known that Derrida became attached to showing how the one and the other condition themselves and so on this basis could be deconstructed by *différ-a-nce*—inclined toward transcendence—which overcomes the dialectic itself.

But Deleuze knows the tricks of this dialectic just as well.

Now what can weigh *différance*? Is it relative in some way to philosophy and its circle, or does it really escape it, moving beyond difference in Deleuze's sense as complementary to repetition? How is this classical antinomy constituted or displaced? What means does Derrida make use of to apparently perform better than Deleuze on this point? Derrida effectively constitutes the Logos as a hierarchy with linguistic means (*Sa* and *Sé*, or signifier and signified), and then he inverts this hierarchy, which is unable to leave the philosophical circle, but he is not content merely to aggravate this inversion in the name of the withdrawal of the signifier—that would be to remain at the level of a priori or within the philosophical circle. He treats signifying difference as a One that invests the *Sa* and withdraws this *différ-a-nce* from logocentrism or places it on the edge of it. The signifier, as suspended from the One, then becomes an alterity that dislocates the circle of the logos and even deconstructs Deleuzian difference, which this new operator now claims to be able to generate, so without completely destroying the amplified and displaced philosophical circle, composed of fragments from now on. For our part we shall retain this excess of the transcendent over the transcendental, even over the Nietzscheanism of Deleuze, an excess that from my perspective is (and is meant to be) Judaic in its origins and, in the name of a religious pathos, intends to overcome philosophy's logocentrism or the transcendental that it displaces. Does Derrida have an advantage over Deleuze? Or not necessarily because of the means it was obtained? Deleuze now has, from our perspective, the advantage over Derrida by being grounding not upon religion but upon science, though certainly still thermodynamic, to pierce the philosophical circle; moreover, he retains the philosophical transcendental that Derrida deconstructs or pulls to pieces.

What is the value of this mellowed antinomy between our two kinds of Différ-e/a-nce? Can we take the best, meaning polemical, point between these two positions to resolve this antinomy, the transcendental of Deleuze and his appeal to physical science, but do we risk then remaining within the philosophical circle because of an insufficiently "advanced" or "revolutionary" science? And Derrida's point, the excess of the transcendent this time over the transcendental, a transcendent also sustained by a science, though it is only linguistics, and which risks coming to a pathos that is more or less secretly religious? This antinomy is first that of philosophy (of Spinoza) and religion (here another Judaism . . .), and finally it comes down to or concentrates onto science as thermodynamic and as linguistic, meaning to the level of the a priori, and then emigrates into the transcendental that it retains or that it even deconstructs. To posit an absolute transcendent would come back to the one with a religious act, but with his Nietzschean thermodynamics, Deleuze is not very effective and lacks a more contemporary and effective science. This is why we will not give our voice to either those who rely on the religious or those who rely on thermodynamics to break or regulate the philosophical circle. We need another science, more effective than linguistics and thermodynamics, against the circle of the Logos.

The transcendental must be conserved as correlated with a transcendent capable of sustaining it by determining it and maybe by overdetermining it without pulling the philosophical logos to pieces, by placing it in reserve instead so as finally to be able to rethink anew the relations of philosophizing humanity and the Universe such as this sought-after science would give a new access to. These are the conditions which, in displacing it and renewing it, pose the problem of philosophy and science. In thus posing the problem, it all becomes clear. The antinomy of our two philosophers is played out in philosophy, or more exactly at its edge and on the possibility of exceeding it, and will require a scientific means to really exceed the circle, but we will follow neither Deleuze nor Derrida even if they point to the way. In any case, it will be a conjugation of science (but which one?) and philosophy, once religion is rejected, regardless of whether it is paganism or Judaism. It is here that our autonomy comes to an end if we push it beyond its techniques of implementation within the circle of philosophy despite everything traditional. How, then, can we make the final step, the one that we need to make: that of leaving the philosophical circle, its diameter or its transcendental amplitude, but with a step that does not deny it or that would begin by reducing and bringing low its sufficiency in order, then, to better save it and amplify it? We retain just the necessary cooperation of the transcendental and science as the transcendent that our two philosophers both recognized as necessary: Deleuze to consider the transcendental, but by assigning it to the guardianship exercised by science for the Universe, but unfortunately an "outdated" or "superseded" [*dépassée*] science that conserves the Copernican revolution, Derrida to deconstruct it by way of the transcendent, but nonscientifically. To leave this philosophical antimony "with honors" or "honorably," meaning with the aid of and in agreement with science, it is necessary to find an unquestionable scientific instance whose transcendence will be capable of dominating the philosophical transcendental without denying it absolutely, only to limit it in order, then, to amplify it—deepening, on one hand, the gap of withdrawal or aggravating it and, on the other, proportionally intensifying the amplitude of excess or the rebound. Inscribing transcendental philosophy in or through the transcendent Universe is possible, but not with the Platonic or even Newtonian Universe or Cosmos—it would at best be the Copernican revolution. But it is possible with quantum physics, with great benefits for the transcendental or the philosophical, more fundamental and even universal, and the transcendence of which will be capable of determining the philosophical transcendental. Maybe, then, it is a matter of an anti- or post-Copernican revolution, another understanding of non-Copernicanism that radicalizes and transmutes the amplitude of the circle.

We are looking for a new concept of the transcendental and of its overdetermination by the quantum and so by the transcendent, which would not allow for the Newtonian context such as philosophy appropriated it. A new topology or economy, known as "Reminscience," allows for the edifice of thought to be reconstructed by displacing philosophy and submitting it to the quantum, so always to the Universe. But this new relation to a non-mythical and non-philosophical Universe modifies the place and function of philosophy that allows it to leave the contemporary antinomy, and guards philosophy as central and principal without denying it or deconstructing it, but displaces it into the general organizing diagram of thought. This organizing diagram is Marxian, as a dissociation and a new unity of the principal and the fundamental, of (empirco/generico-real) class struggle and the real—an entirely relative disassociation, since it is understood as overdetermination of the transcendental by the transcendence of the Universe. This is the reversal of the Newtonian philosophism, exaggerated in its magnitude by the remaining geocentric narcissism found within Newtonian physics. In other words, starting with Derrida and Deleuze, we must question the Copernican revolution and seek its contemporary elaboration, a quantum revolution or one that is Planckian, and so on. The antinomy of our two D and D is the distant outcome, the last fruit of the Newtonian revolution and the excessive place of philosophy. It is in this capacity that we fight it and substitute the quantum for it.

Demonstrating that the ground and object of the No and the Yes change within this non-Nietzschean transvaluation of philosophy as transcendental axis and spinal column of the body of thought, now overdetermined by the real, a transcendental which was the circle encompassing all of the real, we now divide up into two spheres instead of making it a unique sphere like the Greeks, including Plato, also did. The PPS is abased or torn away from its sufficiency in the mythical Universe, which guaranteed it badly or with an illusion. But it is deracinated from the mythical soil also to be in other respects, and for a second time, no longer transvalued or amplified as the unique ground that it claimed to be, so without denying every philosophical foundation, but insofar as it now shares the foundation as a common work of the principal with the fundamental. It is its principal aspect that forms a collapse, a breakdown, with the fundamental aspect of the real as basis. This is a new function for philosophy, and it signifies its abasement as a condition for its fundamental raising up by its real overdetermination. The solution is in the Marxian style without being economistic or Marxist. Philosophy remains fundamental for generic experience, but it is twice relativized, the first time by its object as human experience "in the world" where it is invested, the second time through its being connected with the quantum, so this is the transcendental determined by the transcendent. Therefore an anti-Copernican revolution is necessary against the Copernicans and transcendental Kant and Newton, or at least partially against Kant. We often use Kantian weapons, but by partially reversing the PPS, which is more complex than the simple or formal transcendental as a "transcendental imagination," and the simplicity of which will be replaced by a new organization of Reminscience.

4

The Philosophical Problem of the Demiurgic Dream as Inherently Humanist

Katerina Kolozova

The "Third Person Perspective"

I argue that Marx's "humanism" is not juxtaposed to his method and project of political economy as developed in *Capital, Volumes I–III.* Instead of with Althusser, who propelled the antihumanist thesis on the basis of what he identified as an "epistemic break" in Marx, I concur with Michel Henry that it is a forced interpretation ungrounded in Marx's own declarations about his theoretical project and, more importantly, in his own text.[1] The humanism designed for the species-being of humanity is rid of philosophy and, therefore, of the Enlightenment humanist project. Marx's humanism is nonhumanist, and the prefix serves the same function as it does in the case of François Laruelle's non-philosophy: it grounds itself in the transcendental of the human as determined by the reality of humanity, that materially determined reality of a species of "objects" called human, rather than philosophical figurations of it. The species that is *object* of study determines the process of inquiry, and the thinking subject acts from a "third person" position. This desubjectivized position for which Marx argues does not resemble the "objective subject" of positivism, as it is nonsubjective. Certainly it is a position assumed by a "subject" or an "agency" or a "self," but is a subject that, in the process of scientific and philosophical inquiry, sees itself as an object too, rather than the other way around (seeing the object of study as a subject and from its assumed "subjective" position, a point to which we shall return). Marxian method seeks to establish itself as scientific rather than philosophical.

The subject of scientific enquiry is "depotentialized," as François Laruelle would put it, by way of assuming the task of "cloning the real": it submits itself to the effects of the reality it seeks to explain by first adequately and accurately "coding" the object of study, that is, reproducing it on the plane of the signifying automata (i.e., natural or formal languages). Like the digital coder, the postphilosophical materialist-realist student of the human "species-being" describes or inscribes the object of study into sign or engages a process of its signification. This transposition into a signifying automaton is quite similar to coding, as it lacks criticality, personal views, or any other subjective investment. It lacks interpretation; it does not offer explanation. However, the real can be accurately "cloned," transformed into language and therefore successfully mediated: what it is has been to some extent mediated, as in *idempotence.* It is a tautology: A = A. Only then can the postphilosophical theorist or scientist start asking questions of cause, offer critical interpretation, point to flaws and propose changes in the reality that is the object of study, moved by concrete material needs. The automaton is in the numb tautological reality of transposition; it acts almost as indifferently as the real object of study. However, the home of the automaton and its determination in the last instance is the nonhumanist human, the human without anthropocentrism, that is, without philosophy, which is by definition "egocentric" or, in other words, anthropocentric. It is so because philosophy thinks from the subjective perspective (of humanity): "The self-abstracted entity, fixed for itself, is man as *abstract egoist—egoism* raised in its pure abstraction to the level of thought."[2] The nonhuman permits subjectivation that is nonanthropocentric while being nonetheless grounded in and determined by the reality of the human species-being. This sort of methodological positioning and metaphysical choice or philosophical heresies (that of postphilosophy) permits posthumanism without the philosophical atavism of the anthropocentric myth. Aided by Marx's political materialism, it does not go against the interests of the human species. In other words, such posthumanism affirms the radical humanity in its aspect of the real—or in its materiality—and it also disables human commodification.

The Nonhuman (Including the Machine and the Animal)

The concept of the nonhuman, insofar as it is radically human, allows for positively posthumanist visions of technological development, for political animal studies and practice, and, finally, for a socialist transformation of society. Thus technological development will be envisioned as a process that does not take place by way of commodification of animal species, including the human species. Quite to the contrary: it is put in motion, motivated and mobilized, by a vision of work beyond wage labor and production and exchange without commodification. This is enabled by an approach that is, in its "identity in the last instance" (Laruelle), materialist in the Marxian sense. Let us recall that Marx is wary of the use of the term *materialist* as essentially construed by philosophy and as having meaning only inside philosophy,[3] so he resorts to the notions of "realism" and "physicalism." It is indeed a certain real that is closer to the Lacanian or the Laruellian concept of the real—as that mute and indifferent disruption of language—that Marx insists should determine his science of the "human species" rather than the "material" as defined by its relation to the "ideal" and conditioned by philosophical binarism. The real or the physical precedes concept or meaning insofar as it is neither "pure immanence" nor "life-force"—it is the modus of concreteness, of being out there, a *Gegenstand*.

The Fallacy of Reification

How a society operates with the physical reality or the real is a question of politics and of epistemology: the operation of signification (thought) should refrain from the error of postulating the abstraction as concreteness, as embodied by physicality. Such error is called "reification," *Verdinglichung*, and its consequences are not only epistemic but also political: its key consequence in social reality is "commodity," the cornerstone of capitalist economy and the philosophy of modernity.[4] It is analogous to the "principle of philosophical sufficiency" Laruelle writes about, which produces the founding fallacy of philosophy: the "amphibology" of the real and thought, whereby "Truth" is born, "the real that is more real than the real itself." It is the real enhanced and perfected by the true or reinvented as meaning. Truth is embodied or fetishized (just as monetary value is fetishized through commodities): a thing is elevated into meaning whereby the latter confers "greater reality" to the real devoid of meaning. The meaningless real is nonexistent. Therefore meaning is the only reality.

The Subject as Essentially Philosophical Category

Both Marx and Laruelle argue for a radical reversal of the perspective. The futile pretension to penetrate the real with meaning and fully possess as truth is inexorably humanist and "subjective" in the Marxian sense. The posthumanist project that seeks to realize a goal of this sort is also essentially humanist, philosophical, and capitalist: it contains the projection of human perfection by way of dialectics (of transcending itself as real and physical). It is predicated on the real—not merely the physical—perfecting itself via meaning, sense. Because the real is always subjectivized in philosophy and capitalism, the main phantasm is perfection of human intelligence by way of transcending any naturalness that just weighs it down: a human that has transcended its human imperfections. That will be a real-ization of the true potential of humanity, of its "true nature," arriving to a real determined by truth, a real more real than the real itself. Marx and Laruelle propose a radically different approach to the real (and/or physicality) and to thought (or sign, language): they ought to be affirmed in their unilaterality or unilateral difference, whereby the "meaning" does not perfect the real and the real is indifferent to thought's mediation of it. To accomplish this, the subjective perspective that anthropomorphizes reality needs to be transcended: our language should be fully formalized and start describing the signifying automata, on one side, and the physical reality, on the other, as well as the reality of their mutual interaction.

The Two Main Categories of a Proposed Formal Language: Automata (Natural and Synthetic) and Physicality (Natural and Synthetic)

To study the human reality beyond the subjective and anthropocentric is to assume the thought posture of a third person: it is neither the stance of *sub specie aeternitatis* nor the subject–object amphibology of object-oriented ontology but is beyond the object–subject logic:

> A being which has no object outside itself is not an objective being. A being which is not itself an object for some third being has no being for its *object*; i.e., it is not objectively related. Its being is not objective. A non-objective being is a *non-being*. . . . For this third object I am thus a *different reality* than itself; that is, I am *its* object. Thus, to suppose a being which is not the object of another being is to presuppose that *no* objective being exists. As soon as I have an object, this object has me for an object. But a *non-objective* being is an unreal, non-sensuous thing—a product of mere thought (i.e., of mere imagination)—an abstraction. To be *sensuous*, that is, to be really existing, means to be an object of sense, to be a *sensuous* object, to have sensuous objects outside oneself—objects of one's sensuousness. To be sensuous is to *suffer*.[5]

It is a laborious effort to describe reality by signifying it, by inscribing it, via scripture for which a language is required. The language is automaton, and Saussure has explained successfully how. A similar model of postulating an automaton of signification has been employed by Alan Turing: finite automata both Saussure and Turing have studied rely on what I will tentatively call "unilateral binarism." The elements in the binary operate via unilateral difference and do not constitute "a meaning" but rather a physical effect that serves to convey "a meaning" or the movement of the signifying chain (language). The "material"—or "physical," as Marx would put it instead—rules of inscription or of coding produce the abstract effect of "cloning the real" and its derivations, such as meaning and truth. The automaton itself is grounded in the "senseless real": in the material "logic" of phonetics, cognitive and physical underpinnings of morphology, the tape and the head and the instructions that move them. The finite automata are moved, as Saussure said, from the "concrete to the abstract":

> For the first time we have broken away from abstraction. Now for the first time we have found the concrete, irreducible units that occupy a place and correspond to a bent in the spoken chain: *p* was nothing except an abstract unit linking the common characters of *p*> and *p*<, the only units that actually exist. In the same way, the still higher abstraction of "labiality" links together *P, M and B*. We may speak of P as if it were a zoological species; there are male and female representatives of the species, but there is no ideal specimen. Before, we had been singling out and classifying the abstractions; but we had to go beyond the abstract to reach the concrete. Phonology made a great mistake in considering abstractions real units without examining more carefully the definition of the unit.[6]

The value exchange system—or the market—is also moved endlessly by the same founding structure of unilateral binary producing the endless chain of M-C-M-C-M-C-M > M′. Yet the result of this simple and physical rule, of this senseless tautology of the real, is an entire "universe of meaning" called capitalism. *The finite automata or languages are formalizations of the material reality of signification.* Thus not only does physical reality support the finite automata but the act of signification itself constitutes a material reality or a "senseless real."

Thought, or the reality of transcendence (of the real or the material), is itself an artifice or a *technē* of mediation, of transposition of the real. By way of emulating the real through sign, the automaton seeks to clone the real: the natural language and the digital do not mirror the real; they enact mimesis of the real in physical reality. Philosophy, however, seeks to be a perfect reflection of the outside or the surface of the real. Language, insofar as it is *technē*, is much less ambitious than philosophy: it does not seek to grasp, possess, and emanate the "true nature" of anything; it emulates it inside the set of rules of a finite automaton of signification. The transposition of the real into the automaton is never complete, and the glaring remainder is acceptable when it comes from a scientific and artistic posture of thought. Commonsense posture and philosophy are disturbed by a fundamental sense of anxiety about the remainder: it is caused by the subject's enjoyment in the self-sufficient universe of the automaton, and the unstoppable pleasure principle that inhabits it, which refuses to accept arbitrariness, contingency, and finitude as the basis for its infinite sequence.

Philosophy precedes and paves the way for the capitalist model of society weaponized in the great metaphysical war for erasing the Remainder on an ontological level: value and sign fetishized as commodity will replace materiality, and the supermachine will supersede the "dumb real" by creating "smart real" or "real with a meaning" (the philosophical dream). This is, however, a contradiction in terms: the real is supposed to be senseless while language or thought transposes it and thus produces sense. They constitute a dyad of nonrelation, a dyad of unilaterality. The more perfect an automaton is, the more perfect is the transposition and the plane of transcendence. However, this does not mean perfection of the real in any of its material instantiations (nature, body, real economy)—they remain indifferent to the concept of "perfection." The affirmation of the radical dyad and its internal unilaterality is ultimately a scientific, non-philosophical, Marxian but also structuralist stance. To render or reveal the real as redundant, to reduce the material reality to resource for exploitation and to declare the body as obsolete, is the philosophical–capitalist phantasm realized as "postmodernism."

The automaton of value exchange (market) and technological automata are, on the other hand (unlike the real), endowed with the tendency to perfect themselves. I do not have in mind "machines that learn" but the tendency of the signification or the automaton to perfect itself through ever greater formalization of language and speed of computing. This process, however, does not lead to exposing or correcting the imperfections of the real—it does not have any "ontological desires." The real, as we said, is indifferent to thought's attempts at mediation, including the autoperfecting automaton. The human and humanist subject dream such dreams, and through philosophy those dreams enter some of the grand obsessions of contemporary political-economic and technological projects, such as AI or the total financialization of the economy. *To complement biology with technology is a scientific and political project grounded in materialist epistemology. To seek to "transcend" biology by technology is a philosophical and humanist dream.* After all, the automaton is indifferent to such desires, whereas its "perfection" is mere further formalization of language leaving behind the residuals of common sense and philosophy.

The automaton of the capitalist society, the language of its ideology, is affected by the philosophical dream in question, which is enabled by the fact that the subjects of this automaton are not merely subjects but also agents of the species-being of humanity. The species-being is a physical reality, materiality inhabited by automata. The human species-being, the individual and collective self and the objective reality, is indeed "posthuman": it is a hybrid of organic and inorganic physicality, on one hand, the automata of natural and digital languages, on the other, blending and producing a world of philosophy or capitalism. The species-being is construed as this radical dyad, a duality established by unilateral constituents. It also branches out into ever more elaborate structures and multiplies endlessly.

Philosophy is the product of the drive to unite the elements of the dyad, to reduce the dyad to a unity, to smooth out the rough surface of hybridity with a glaring senselessness at the center of it (the real that escapes transposition into meaning). It operates on the plane of the transcendental, but it is moved by the anxiety of the "nonhuman," that asymmetric composition of physicality, animality, and signification in its embarrassing mechanicity. It is the remainder of senselessness that escapes transformation into thought, truth, or sense and that exposes the "artificiality" of that plane and the procedure of transposition. *The great effort of philosophy to erase the traces of embarrassment has morphed into rationality and rationalism, a philosophical fetish embedded in science.* Scientific practice is indifferent to the "values" of rationalism—it operates according to an ever-perfecting formal language that cannot distinguish between "Reason" (Ratio) and God, or art, crafts, or all that is *technē*, or the core of social practices.

Yet again, the type of thought we call philosophy and its materialization as capitalist political and economic order define the "universe of meanings" we inhabit and subjectivize. It is an operation of language, but language does not "ascribe meaning." Language is an indifferent machine. Thought is moved by something that escapes the automaton of natural language or the formal language of science, something that overwhelms it. That "something," in Laruelle's vocabulary, is the person-in-person, the human self insofar as the real that constitutes the "radical subjectivity."[7] The pretension to substitute the awkward real with a smooth surface of signification is philosophical. To submit to the real as the determining instance of these processes is to assume the postphilosophical, Marxian, and non-philosophical posture of thought. The submission in question entails affirmation of the radical dyad of nonhumanity composed of the automaton and the physical as unilateral elements of the binary. It is indeed a "depotentialized" position, as Laruelle argues.[8] The *technē* of knowledge, the craft of signification, is not ontologized in postphilosophy; it remains a laborious practice of "coding," "cloning," and being a body (both natural and synthetic). That reality must serve a meaning, that the real must be reducible to truth, is the reasoning and desire that underpins philosophy. That the material "resources" of this planet must be transformed in value is the reasoning and desire that underpins capitalism. They establish perfectly analogous equations: real = truth > material = value. To overcome philosophy is to overcome capitalism, and that can be done only by affirming the radical dyad of the physical and the automaton and the nonhuman that hosts them.

The Urgency of Introducing Radical Metaphysics into Technopolitical and Economic Debates

Metaphysics without Philosophy

The questions "What is the self?" "What is life worth living for?" "Is the machine ultimately material or ideal (conceptual)?" "What is rationality?" "What is human development?" and "Is an exit from capitalism possible?" could all be called philosophical. If we radicalize their contents, if we establish "the identity in the last instance" of what is at stake in the questions, will they necessarily be philosophical? Aspects of each could be answered through individual sciences (cognitive psychology, biology, economics), but to address the "determination in the last instance" of the question, one would have to resort to "philosophical material," as Laruelle calls it. To operate with concepts or "transcendental material" of philosophy, but in a manner that is rid of the "principle of philosophical sufficiency," is to do non-philosophy. When referring to the "principle of philosophical sufficiency," Laruelle refers to the problem of amphibology between the truth and the real as presented earlier. Or put differently, philosophy posits the real, interprets the outside reality in line with it, and discards anything that "does not make sense" according to the posited real. It comes down to the problem of the real = fiction and fiction = real, as already discussed, whereby the truth "becomes more real than the real itself." Despite the multiplicity of philosophical schools, the amphibology exemplified in the concept of *to ôn* (the Being) is what underpins all of them and determines the terminological apparatus or the language used across different philosophical schools. Thus abandoning this principle, and with it the narcissistic auto-referentiality of philosophy, situates the subject that theorizes as non-philosophical.

Marx's study of the species-being of humanity constitutes a science that deals with value production and the relation of value to the material reality—it also operates with philosophical material, but not as philosophy. Philosophy unavoidably yields idealism, even when materialism is its doctrine.[9] Following Marx and Laruelle, I argue that these questions can be answered by use of "philosophical material," but in a postphilosophical manner.

The postphilosophical approach I suggest here consists of the complete formalization of the question and the language to pursue it. It should treat the material at hand (the conceptual material originating in philosophy) as material and as matter, if you will, approaching it along the vector "from the concrete to the abstract," establishing a homology in method with Saussure. By referring to the latter, I have in mind the passage on the "concrete" and the "abstract" phoneme, quoted earlier, and Saussure's declared goal to "break away from abstraction." Such a goal is possible only if the approach is unequivocally materialist:

> To give an account of what takes place within groups, there should be a science of sound that would treat articulatory movements like algebraic equations: a binary combination implies a certain number of mechanical and acoustical elements that mutually condition each other; the variation of one has a necessary and calculable repercussion on the others.[10]

A similar trajectory is undertaken in Marx's *Capital*, in which an exact understanding of the "concrete," a description of empirical data and explication of its patterns, leads to discoveries about the laws that govern the exchange of goods or the market more generally and, finally, to the abstractions of "commodity" and "value." The examination and problematization of the relation between the material and the abstract, between use-value and exchange-value, nonetheless requires mobilization of "philosophical material." The problem of the tautology of value reproducing value, the detachment of the automaton of the market from the physical reality, is a metaphysical question, and as such it should be radicalized—treated as material or real, as a real abstraction, following Marx's model. Instead of discounting metaphysics, one could formalize the language of inquiry while abandoning the principle of philosophical circularity or self-sufficiency. Formalization does not necessarily imply computing or closed automaton. The formal languages of postphilosophy allow for metaphors and poesy as they allow the remainder that escapes signification. They can be simultaneously rigorously formulaic and yet poetic, such as in the following example from Marx:

> In simple circulation, C-M-C, the value of commodities attained at the most a form independent of their use-values, *i.e.*, the form of money; but that same value now in the circulation M-C-M, or the circulation of capital, suddenly presents itself as an independent substance, endowed with a motion of its own, passing through a life-process of its own, in which money and commodities are mere forms which it assumes and casts off in turn. Nay, more: instead of simply representing the relations of commodities, it enters now, so to say, into private relations with itself. It differentiates itself as original value from itself as surplus-value; as the father differentiates himself from himself qua the son, yet both are one and of one age: for only by the surplus-value of £10 does the £100 originally advanced become capital, and so soon as this takes place, so soon as the son, and by the son, the father, is begotten, so soon does their difference vanish, and they again become one, £110.[11]

The description—or transposition into signification—of the reality observed is conducted in a way that is very similar to what Laruelle would call the "cloning of the real."[12] The more the "code" seeks to emulate the processes in the real, the more it becomes formal, rid of valorization and "libidinal investment." Marx uses natural language to clone the real, but the stance is one rid of valorization, judgment, or projections of philosophical phantasms. The more sterile it is, the more formal it is (despite the recourse to natural language). In the end, the interpretation arrives, which is a valorization, a metaphysical choice; for example, commodification introduces alienation, and alienation introduces dehumanization. The latter is opposite to fulfilling the "human essence," and that is a position on a metaphysical matter.[13] The more formalized the postphilosophical analysis is, the more scientific and metaphysical it is at the same time. The metaphor of the son begetting the father is the metaphor of the antinaturalism of capitalism—not merely beyond naturalism, but simply antinaturalism and perversion, which is at the core of its violence. The metaphor is poetic; its function is metaphysical even as it encapsulates the scientific point. Thus postphilosophy, both Marxian science and Laruellian non-philosophy, should not just draw its material of analysis from philosophy but, by way of use of a particular material, from philosophy, analyze the "outside," the material reality we inhabit in its *unheimlich* aspect of the real. And in the overall approach to more complex realities subject to analysis, we should not only resort to postphilosophy but also allow in other sciences. If we are submitting to the real rather than the principle of philosophy's sufficiency, we shall allow biology, cognitive psychology, and, in some parts, mathematics, quantum theory, or, for that matter, other sciences too.

Economy, Economics, and Its Postphilosophical Aspects

Marx has posited the problem of commodity fetishism and of value estranged from its material use (or "use-value") as both a problem of economic unsustainability and a philosophical (or rather postphilosophical) and epistemic problem. The postphilosophical epistemic problem, if further formalized by way of operating with its "identity in the last instance" (Laruelle), comes down to a metaphysics of the "double estrangement" (I will explain this notion later) and the estrangement of value engendering value that will result in a self-sufficient "bubble" of growth on the "stock exchange" (Marx) in no correlation to or in disregard for the real material economy.[14] That will lead to a necessary collapse of the system, argues Marx. Whether after such collapse one will try to resurrect the specter of the "credit system economy," or what we now call the "finance economy," or resort to a materialist approach to economic production, what we now call the "real economy," is equally an economic and philosophical or metaphysical decision. To be able to see that the self-sufficient economy of value producing value completely detached from use or materiality is not sustainable is an estimation of economics. However, to determine its consequences for material production, to choose such an angle of analysis, the economist has to take a political and metaphysical position: does the disparaging of physicality matter, politically and economically? Such a question is metaphysical. Yet to answer it non-philosophically and in a Marxian vein is to answer it scientifically—through the formalization of language and recourse to data coming from the empirical sciences.

Choosing a radically materialist approach rid of philosophy (yet operating with its "transcendental material" when necessary), adopting a posture of thought that submits to the real by way of "cloning it" before deciding of it, is what determines a Marxian analysis of the economic reality. There is no "economic determinism" in Marx, as economy is seen as part of a more complex treatment of materiality, the real, physicality, and the body. Economy is the determination in the last instance of how the species-being of humanity creates and reproduces its social reality. The analysis moves from the concrete to the abstract, just as it does in Saussure's structuralist account of language, but it does not imply that human reality is reducible to economy, just as human language is not reduced in Saussure to a set of phonemes. Thus, although the line of analysis begins with and relies on "cloning," the material reality of human social reproduction, that is, economy, there is no implication that it projects the "truth of human reality." That is why Marx's approach is postphilosophical or even non-philosophical in the Laruellian sense: it does not merge the real and truth, they do not constitute an amphibology—the real is not true or truth, nor the other way around. Their relationship is a nonrelationship: it is unilateral. It is a line of analysis, not a mirror of the hidden truth of human essence. Philosophy mirrors. Science explains through "cloning according to the syntax of the real."[15] It is very similar to coding as in computer languages or to signifying as in natural languages: they do not reflect any essence of any reality; they merely transpose it into signs.

The choices we make on the basis of such scientifically coded realities are political, economic, and, finally, metaphysical (or of radicalized postphilosophy). The choice relates to the modes of production but is moved by a "material interest" (Marx): that the real and material ought to benefit the sense and sensation of well-being, which is not only bodily but also "spiritual" *(geistlich)*, is what motivates the choice (and the sensation is material insofar as "sensuous," as Marx puts it). It is a choice between value as detached from materiality and materiality signified as value via language or the transcendental plane. To be able to recognize and signify the two and form language of them is to enact metaphysics. Let us remind ourselves that Marx does recognize and affirm what we will call the radical and unavoidable abstraction or alienation: signification and exchange of value are unavoidable parts of the human species-being. However, their double estrangement through commodification is the philosophical, metaphysical, economic, and political error of capitalism. Similar are the errors of philosophy, as we find out in his critiques of Hegel, Feuerbach, and other philosophers who have attempted but failed at the *Ausgang* from philosophy. This particular point in Marx's arguments has been further developed through the concept of "real abstraction" that we find in Sohn Rethel's *Intellectual and Manual Labor: A Critique of Epistemology* (1978).

The Nonhuman, the Animal, and the Exploitation of the Animal

The physical and the material, or the real, in the human species is affirmed in its unilateral difference from the plane of values and signs, from the transcendental. While they establish a radical dyad, or a binary of unilaterally positioned elements,[16] the radical constructedness is affirmed: to the level of the transcendental belong economic and other forms of value production and the entire realm of signifying activities, including technology. Marx claimed that we are "posthuman" before the poststructuralists and before Donna Haraway. However, unlike the other posthumanists, and very much like Donna Haraway, he insisted that one element of its construction was our naturalness or animality. To exploit a human for capital is to rid it of its realness insofar as it embodies physicality, insofar as it is an animal—to reduce it to an element in the automaton of value production. Dehumanization, as Marx criticizes it, is in fact deanimalization.[17] But what is more important and makes the dichotomy between the human and animal false, or the argument insufficiently formalized, is that dematerialization and derealization are at stake. Thus dematerialization and derealization are synonymous in our argument, following Marx, who operates only with the notions of reality and physicality rather than materiality. In his analysis of the species-being of humanity, physicality and the real are synonymous. In other types of analysis, such as the opposition of use-value and surplus-value, he does not refer to the physicality or bodily reality of humanity, nor does he refer to it when contrasting material or real production against the complete financialization of the economy that he calls the "credit system economy."[18]

The aspect of the human that is "physical but also spiritual" (although "spirituality" is still determined by "muscles and nerves") is what is estranged, depressed, and exploited—and on the basis of this depression, the automation of commodity production takes place.[19] Commodity is produced by the estrangement of use-value from surplus-value, or simply by the estrangement of materiality from value. In a second movement, this pure value is seemingly embodied or "materialized" as money and private property. Wage labor is also estranged from its materiality by way of considering it abstract, "labor in general" measured in money or as having a certain value. One becomes an abstract unit in a process that derealizes one, insofar as automation or signification occurs, which is by definition abstraction and opposite to the real.

To fight derealization is to fight for rehabilitation of the physical or animal as the aspect of humanity that is exploited, on which violence is exerted to accelerate its function in automated value production. The form of violence it suffers is sometimes literally physical, such as hunger, poor health, homelessness, contemporary slavery, and work in sweatshops, child labor, and underpaid women's labor. It more often takes place through the violence of the automation of labor itself. Sometimes it is precisely the negation of physicality that constitutes and inflicts violence: the reduction of labor force to a unit in the automation of commodity value production. In addition to the derealization that happens through wage labor (also rent), the transformation of the human body into a resource for capital, for example, the trafficking of human beings and the trade in surrogacy (rent of wombs) and organs, is another form of exploitation of the physical for the purposes of industrial production.

The treatment of the human body in this late stage of capitalism is no "posthumanization"; it is nothing that transcends the "inferior," animal-like nature of humanity. Quite to the contrary, it is the reduction to animality as resource for capital or for pure value (cleaned of materiality) rather than full technologization that perpetuates the M-M tautology at an ever greater speed. *The exploited animal, regardless of whether human or not, sustains the market and the ideology of pure, dematerialized value.* The exploited and devalued prelingual animal is what sustains modern philosophy too. The "assembly line" as the prototype of automated human labor is a model developed in the meat industry, or to be more precise, in the American slaughterhouses of the late nineteenth century: the line of fully automated human labor of disassembling the animal body is the perfect metaphor for what sustains the philosophical and capitalist phantasm of a universe of pure value. The purity in question, of course, refers to detachment, independence from and superiority over the physical and, in particular, its embarrassing aspect of animality. That living matter, the animal, is the embarrassing reminder of human animality, nonexclusivity, slowness, dependence (on nature), decay, and mortality. It is exploited because indeed the exploiter deems it inferior to its valorization (as money, as progress, as history—any form of valorization), because the capitalist treats the material as the philosopher treats the real.

The human body in its aspect of animality, or by way of reducing it to an animal, is formatted for capitalist exploitation. Insofar as it is viewed as animal or in its aspect of animality, it is subjected to full annihilation and transformation into value exchanged via the signifying automaton of the market. Capitalism perpetuates the holocaust of animals as the basis of existence. Women, the human animals that menstruate and whose bodies are objects of endless ideological war (over which they hardly have any sovereignty in the greatest part of our neoliberal planet), women as animals are part of the holocaust. As are the children reduced to animals—those stripped of the surplus-value called "human dignity"—through their exploitation and practical slavery in sweatshops. The animals, including the human animals stripped of agency or recognition as participants in a debate on humans as animals, are the main resource for the capitalist holocaust of materiality. On the ashes of this holocaust, the projection of a universe of pure values (of sign . . .) is built.

A Socialist and Feminist Machine

The machine or automation as an independent, self-enveloped, and self-sufficient universe of signification or value production is "capitalism out of joint." Value is produced out of value, sign out of sign; phallus engenders phallus. The capitalist market, as already elaborated, constitutes yet another exchange system of signification or—simply—language. The capitalist signifying chain perpetually engages in transforming not only the physical but the real as category into a resource for signification:

> The development of the means of labour into machinery is not an accidental moment of capital, but is rather the historical reshaping of the traditional, inherited means of labour into a form adequate to capital. The accumulation of knowledge and of skill, of the general productive forces of the social brain, is thus absorbed into capital, as opposed to labour, and hence appears as an attribute of capital.[20]

The capitalist creation of surplus-value takes on a life of its own. It is the endless chatter of signifying, unstoppable in its schizophrenic split from the material or, rather, the real. The capitalist exploitative relation to physicality insofar as it is conceived as the real *intends* to be indifferent, unilateral, while in fact it remains relational: it has to *posit* the physical as "mere material" to treat it indifferently and as nothing more than resource. Thus the indifference is not immanent, as it is in the real, but rather conditioned by a proposition (and decision) as to what the "true nature of the material" is. The metaphysical anxiety springing from the fact that a postulation is not the same as the real is soothed with a classical philosophical move: the postulate itself is accorded the status of the real. Its latest authoritative mutation is that of constructivism, which annuls the real (because of its irrelevance), reduces it to sheer "noise," declares it nonexistent insofar as it is outside the human reach of manipulation.

Some of the most influential feminist Marxist philosophers have advocated technological progress as the main avenue of women's liberation. Shulamith Firestone claimed that the social subjugation of women is the result of their biological vulnerability.[21] Donna Haraway has argued that the exploitation of the animal is the cornerstone of capitalism and that a feminist-socialist emancipation must go through the liberation of the physical. According to Haraway, technology is the creation and property of militaristic and capitalist patriarchy establishing a hierarchical binary with the biological or the animal, whereby the latter is subjected to and exploited by the former.[22] To liberate the animal, therefore, implies liberation of the physical and, hence, of women from their biological vulnerability. Rosi Braidotti advocated a thesis about animal–machine continuity in her *Metamorphoses* (2002), only to build on it the materialist defense of life *(zoē)* from capitalist commodification and exploitation elaborated in her later book *The Posthuman*.[23]

A continuity between the physical and the technological constituting what Haraway terms the "cyborg" is the form of subjectivation endowed with the potential for socialist and feminist liberation. The first condition for the appearance of the cyborg, Haraway argues, is the hybridization of the animal and technology:

> And many people no longer feel the need for such a separation; indeed, many branches of feminist culture affirm the pleasure of connection of human and other living creatures. Movements for animal rights are not irrational denials of human uniqueness; they are a clear-sighted recognition of connection across the discredited breach of nature and culture. The cyborg appears in myth precisely where the boundary between human and animal is transgressed. Far from signalling a walling off of people from other living beings, cyborgs signal disturbingly and pleasurably tight coupling. Bestiality has a new status in this cycle of marriage exchange.[24]

Bestiality means both animality and monstrosity. The cyborg is a monstrous figure preconditioned by a politics firmly asserting continuity between nature and culture, body (or the organic) and technology, animal and human, argues Haraway.[25] A feminist and a socialist politics is necessarily "cyborg politics," argues Haraway, as is Marx's species-being of humanity radically construed as animal or natural and profoundly technological (productive or creative) insofar as it is social: "Cyborg politics is the struggle for language and the struggle against perfect communication, against the one code that translates all meaning perfectly, the central dogma of phallogocentrism. That is why cyborg politics insist on noise and advocate pollution, rejoicing in the illegitimate fusions of animal and machine."[26] The prerequisite of Haraway's, Braidotti's, and Firestone's aim of a feminist materialist and socialist revolution through technology, is, let us underscore, the emancipation of the body from the brutal exploitation on the side of the philosophical phantasm of Ratio(nality). As noted at the beginning, rationality and rationalism are philosophical fetishes, whereas scientific thought is more humble in its ambition and perception of itself: it exacts the laborious task of "coding" the real—or "cloning the real," as Laruelle would put it—to produce formal language that engenders questions that can be theorized. The defining capitalist and/or philosophical dualism dictates that rationality is more than a mere cognitive faculty—it is the main constituent of its own ontology insofar as rationality is in and for itself the purpose. If we are to pursue a feminist-socialist project established in fidelity with Marx's oeuvre, we should overcome the founding contradiction of capitalism consisting in the split between "abstract activity and a belly." The brutal indifference of "abstraction"/value vis-à-vis the "belly"/use creates an unsustainable division.

Sexuality and reproduction are central coordinates of bodily experiences. Body or physicality in Marx is the instantiation of the real or physicality *par excellence*. That is why I do not see a possibility of a socialist feminist emancipation without it resorting to technology as the means to emancipate the female body and social subject from its reproductive vulnerabilities. A Marxian vision of technology's feminist emancipating force would consist in arguing for its prosthetic function instead of an ontological vision of it—technology does not seek to exploit or annihilate the physical but to aid the human species-being where it is most vulnerable. We should understand the term *prosthesis* in its etymological sense, referring to its status of extension with respect to the physical rather than its substitute or the ontological perfection of "inferior nature." Instead of relying on the philosophical interpretations of technology, which are unavoidably determined by the hierarchical oscillations between "reason" and "body," a Marxist understanding of technology should operate with its prephilosophical meaning of *technē* and, therefore, its prosthetic essence. Anchoring technology in the real and in the physical is in direct opposition to the self-sufficient universe of the automation that defines capitalism, both as metaphysics and as economy. In itself, technology does not vouch for such—or any—emancipation. A political program can determine its social function, not the other way around.

Though the sex class system may have originated in fundamental biological conditions, this does not guarantee, once the biological basis of their oppression has been swept away, that women and children will be freed. On the contrary, the new technology, especially fertility control, may be used against them to reinforce the entrenched system of exploitation.[27]

The idea that science and technology possess some inherent laws of functioning and self-regulation that are independent from ideology, philosophy, and economy resembles the naive (neo)liberal belief that the capitalist economy is based on laws that constitute a nature in its own right or that it emulates nature itself. The metaphysical presupposition that technology's development moves along a curve of infinity displays unchecked "philosophical spontaneity" (Laruelle): it is the product of the inherently philosophico-theological opposition between the immortality of reason and the finitude of nature and physicality. If we are to establish a socialist and feminist critique of contemporary trends in technological development, moving beyond this type of metaphysics and beyond philosophy is the indispensable grounding gesture for such a project. The nonhumanist human or the nonhuman constituted of the machine–body physicality, on one hand, and the signifying automaton, on the other hand, if affirmed in its brutal and senseless reality as the radical dyad, allows for a historical-materialist conceptualization of technology and its role in the future post-capitalist society.

Notes

1. Michel Henry, *Marx: A Philosophy of Human Reality* (Bloomington: Indiana University Press, 1983), 10.
2. Karl Marx, "Critique of Hegel's Philosophy in General," in *Economic and Philosophical Manuscripts 1844* (Moscow: Progress, 2000), from the online version of the Marxist Internet Archive, https://www.marxists.org/archive/marx/works/download/pdf/Economic-Philosophic-Manuscripts-1844.pdf.
3. Karl Marx, first thesis in *Theses on Feuerbach* (Moscow: Progress, 2002), from the *Marxist Internet Archive*, https://www.marxists.org/archive/marx/works/1845/theses/theses.htm; Marx, "Critique of Hegel's Philosophy in General."
4. Georg Lukács, *History and Class Consciousness*, trans. Rodney Livingstone (Cambridge, Mass.: MIT Press, 1971), https://www.marxists.org/archive/lukacs/works/history/hcc05.htm; Gajo Petrović, "Reification," in *A Dictionary of Marxist Thought*, ed. Tom Bottomore et al. (Cambridge, Mass.: Harvard University Press, 1983), 463–65.
5. Marx, "Critique of Hegel's Philosophy in General."
6. Fernand de Saussure, *Course in General Linguistics*, ed. Charles Bally and Albert Reidlinger, trans. Wade Baskin (New York: Philosophical Library, 1959), 53.
7. François Laruelle, *Théorie des étrangers: science des hommes, démocratie, non-psychanalyse* (Paris: Kimé, 1995), 166.
8. Laruelle, *Théorie générale des victimes* (Paris: Fayard, 2012), 30.
9. Marx, first thesis.
10. Saussure, *Course in General Linguistics*, 51.
11. Marx, *Capital, Volume I*, trans. Samuel Moore and Edward Aveling, ed. Frederick Engels (Moscow: Progress, 1995), from the online version of the Marxist Internet Archive, https://www.marxists.org/archive/marx/works/1867-c1/; see also Marx, *Capital, Volume III*, chapter 4, https://www.marxists.org/archive/marx/works/1894-c3/ch04.htm.
12. Laruelle, *Introduction au non-marxisme* (Paris: Presses Universitaires de France, 2000), 47–48, 61.
13. Marx, manuscript 3 in *Economic and Philosophic Manuscripts 1844*.
14. Katerina Kolozova, *Toward a Radical Metaphysics of Socialism: Marx and Laruelle* (Brooklyn, N.Y.: Punctum Books, 2015), 57.
15. Laruelle, *Introduction au non-marxisme*, 46–47.

16. Laruelle, *Philosophie et non-philosophie* (Liège: Pierre Mardaga, 1989), 70.
17. Marx, *Grundrisse: Outlines of the Critique of Political Economy*, trans. Martin Nicolaus (New York: Penguin Books, 1973), 620.
18. Marx, *Capital, Volume 3*, chapter 5.
19. Marx, *Capital, Volume 1*, book 1.
20. Marx, *Grundrisse*, 622.
21. Shulamith Firestone, *The Dialectic of Sex: The Case for Feminist Revolution* (New York: William Morrow, 1970), 10.
22. Donna Haraway, *Simians, Cyborgs and Women: The Reinvention of Nature* (New York: Routledge, 1991), 151.
23. Rosi Braidotti, *Metamorphoses: Toward a Materialist Theory of Becoming* (Cambridge: Polity Press, 2002); Braidotti, *The Posthuman* (Cambridge: Polity Press, 2013), 62.
24. Haraway, *Simians*, 152.
25. Haraway, 150, 155.
26. Haraway, 176.
27. Firestone, *Dialectic of Sex*, 10.

5

Without Priors

Frank B. Wilderson III

The year 1987: two years before I went to South Africa for the first time, and four years before I would go, for five years, to live there. I worked as a guard at the Walker Art Center overlooking downtown Minneapolis and taught creative writing on the weekends and at night, while I licked my wounds from eight ethically bankrupt years as a stockbroker. The first Intifada had just begun in Palestine, and I had a dear friend from Ramallah who was also a guard at the museum. His name was Nabil. Nabil was a photographer who studied at the Minneapolis Institute of Art. But of most importance was the fact that we shared the same politics (revolutionary) and the same star sign (Aries): two people who were often wrong but never in doubt. "If we were in an airplane," Nabil once told me, "and we crashed in the desert and a survivors detail was formed, some people would be tasked with finding water, it would be the job of others to forage for food and firewood, and we would need a team to build a shelter from what could be salvaged from the crash. But you, Frank, you would be one sitting back giving us orders." I didn't spoil the satisfaction he got from the dig by telling him he had mapped onto me traits that were just as applicable to him.

Most of the guards were either artists or writers or students. But only Nabil shared my politics of insurrection. We bonded early and kept our distance from the rest. I told him of my college dreams of going to Zimbabwe and fighting for ZANU/ZAPU or to New York to join Assata Shakur and the Black Liberation Army. Nabil longed to return to Ramallah to make what he thought would be a more meaningful contribution to the Intifada than the talks he gave to moist-eyed Minnesota liberals. He was twenty-five. I was thirty-one. In five years, I would be the same age Frantz Fanon was when he died in the custody of the Central Intelligence Agency (CIA). By the time Fanon died, he had fled Martinique, his native land; joined De Gaulle's army and been wounded fighting the Nazis; completed his internship in psychiatry and medicine; joined the Front de Libération Nationale in the Algerian revolution; and penned four books on revolution and psychoanalysis. I had five years to catch him—a bar set high by my shame-demon. Hubris at low places was where I lived. Much the same was true for Nabil. What a waste, he told me, photographing Scandinavians and loons when I should be back home making bombs. We had different shoulders, but they bore the same weight. I was convinced of this one morning when he came to work smiling, despite the fact that his right eye was slightly bulbous and closed. Last night, he informed me, a friend of mine from Palestine met these two gorgeous women (white, of course, he said, under his breath). I didn't bother to question the "of course" because I wasn't sure that he wasn't wrong. That white beauty goes without saying is the message one is fed all of one's life. To protest to the contrary is like being shortchanged and proclaiming to the person who shortchanged you, "This isn't about money!" Nabil said that he and his friend could have taken them home if three rich Kuwaitis hadn't sauntered into the lounge. When one of the Kuwaitis made a move on the woman Nabil was talking to, Nabil told him, in a kind way, to go back to his booth. The man scoffed and said, "You don't even have your country." But he went back. As the night wore on, the Kuwaitis sent champagne to Nabil's table. Then all three of them approached. They offered to take the women to an exclusive afterparty at a penthouse suite in the suburb of Edina. Just you two, the one Nabil had sent packing said, not the stateless ones. Since they were three and Nabil and his friend were two, they accepted Nabil's offer to discuss the details of the party in the parking lot. Nabil waited for the teeth of the time clock to pierce his employment card, then he put on the blue museum blazer that we all wore, and I followed him into the main gallery. As I passed him to take up my position on the mezzanine, he smiled. “We beat those Kuwaitis until we were tired.” It wasn’t as much bucked horns locked over pride of possession of two forbidden females that sparked the dustup in the parking lot—though that was surely part of it. What seared the flesh on his skin most was the Kuwaitis’ jibe at Nabil’s landlessness. I felt it, too, and thought my loss (whatever I thought was my loss) was analogous to his. I would have beaten them too, I said.

In those days, a high, grassy knoll abutted the building that housed the Walker Art Center. The knoll is gone now, dug out and scraped clean like a root canal. Nabil and I often took our lunch there. In springtime, when the cold breaks and the skies clear, it commands a view of white swans lacing the surface of the lake at Loring Park and distant cars in downtown streets sparkling like sequins in the sun. From that knoll you could see the Basilica of St. Mary’s copper dome corroded by melted snow and driving rain to a blue-green brilliance that once made me think that ruin was the true object of love. The knoll was also a vantage point from which death in the making would be seen. Just below it was the Bottleneck, an intersection where three streets converged into one, a place where some of the most horrifying collisions occurred.

That hill was where Nabil told me about his cousin who, the day before, was killed in Ramallah—blown up while making a bomb. But he wasn’t a suicide bomber. The Israeli occupation had yet to reach such levels as to push the insurgent populace to such tactics. It was an accident. Nabil blamed himself, the way that survivors often do, no matter how near or far in space and time they are from their dead. He survived by being here and not there. Nabil spoke openly as we watched the world below us rush by without even looking up to pay its respects. At one point Nabil spoke of being stopped and searched at Israeli checkpoints. He spoke in a manner that seemed not to require my presence. I hadn’t seen this level of concentration and detachment in him before. That was fine. He was grieving. The shameful and humiliating ways the soldiers ran their hands up and down your body, he said. Then, he said, “but the shame and humiliation ran even deeper if the Israeli soldier was an Ethiopian Jew.”

The earth gave way. The thought that my place in the unconscious of Palestinians fighting for their freedom was the same *dishonorable* place I occupied in the minds of whites in America and Israel chilled me. I gathered enough wits about me to tell him that his feelings were odd, seeing how Palestinians were at war with Israelis, and white Israelis at that. How was it that the people who stole his land and slaughtered his relatives were somehow *less* of a threat in his imagination than Black Jews, the implements of Israeli madness, who sometimes do their dirty work? What, I wondered, silently, was it about Black people (about *me*) that made us so fungible that we could be tossed like salad in the minds of oppressors and oppressed?

I was faced with the realization that in the collective unconscious, the Palestinian insurgence has more in common with Israeli state and civil society than it does with Black people. What they share is a largely unconscious consensus that Blackness is a locus of abjection to be instrumentalized on a whim.[1] At one moment, Blackness is a disfigured and disfiguring phobic phenomenon; at another moment, Blackness is a sentient implement to be joyously deployed for reasons and agendas that have little to do with Black liberation.[2] There I sat, yearning, in solidarity with my Palestinian friend's yearning, for the full restoration of Palestinian sovereignty; mourning, in solidarity with my friend's mourning, over the loss of his insurgent cousin; yearning, that is, for the historical and political *redemption* of what I thought was a violated Commons to which *we both belonged*—when, all of a sudden, my friend reached down into the unconscious of his people and slapped me upside the head with a wet gym shoe: the startling realization that not only was I barred, ab initio, from the denouement of historical and political redemption but the borders of redemption are policed by whites and nonwhites alike and in unison *even as they kill each other.*

It's worse than that. I, as a Black person (if *person, subject, being* are appropriate, because Human is not) am both barred from the denouement of social and historical redemption and *needed* if redemption is to attain any form of coherence. Without the articulation of a common negrophobogenesis that relays between Israeli and Palestinian, the narrative coherence of their bloody conflict would evaporate. My friend's, and his country's women's and men's negrophobogenesis, is the bedrock, the concrete slabs upon which any edifice of Human articulation (whether love or war) is built. Degraded humanity can be frisked by exalted humanity and still remain within the walls of reason; they shake, but they stand. But when one is molested by a *thing* . . .

A mammoth pain swelled in my chest. Nabil and I were antagonists, not because as friends we were mismatched, and not because our politics were incompatible, but because the imago of the Black is "responsible for every conflictual situation."[3] For the libidinal economy that positions the Black imago as a phobogenic object saturates the collective unconscious; it usurps me as an instrument *for*, though never a beneficiary *of*, every nation's woes—even the woes of two nations at war.

For years I had seen myself as a degraded Human, seen my plight as analogous to the plight of Palestinians, Native Americans, and the working class. Now, I understood that analogy was a ruse. I was the foil of Humanity. Humanity looked to me when it was unsure of itself. I let Humanity sigh, in existential relief, "At least we're not him." To quote Saidiya Hartman, "the slave is neither civic man nor free worker but excluded from the narrative of 'we the people' that effects the linkage of the modern individual and the state. . . . The everyday practices of the enslaved occur in the default of the political, in the absence of the rights of man or the assurances of the self-possessed individual, and perhaps even without a 'person,' in the usual meaning of the term."[4]

Black people *embody* (which is different from saying are always willing or allowed to express) a meta-aporia for political thought and action. Blacks do not function as political subjects; instead, our flesh and energies are instrumentalized for postcolonial, immigrant, feminist, LGBT, and workers' agendas. These so-called allies are never *authorized* by Black agendas predicated on Black ethical dilemmas. A Black radical agenda is terrifying to most people on the Left because it emanates from a condition of suffering for which there is no imaginable strategy for redress—no narrative of social, political, or national redemption. This crisis, no, this catastrophe, this realization that I am a sentient being who can't use words like "being" or "person" to describe myself without the scare quotes and the threat of raised eyebrows from anyone within earshot, was crippling.

I was convinced that if a story of Palestinian redemption could be told—its denouement culminating in the return of the land, *a spatial, cartographic redemption*; if a story of class redemption could be told—its denouement culminating in the restoration of the working day so that one stopped working when the labor was enough to produce *use* value, and surplus value was relegated to the dustbin of history, *a temporal redemption*; then there must be a story to be told through which one could redeem the time and place of Black subjugation. I was wrong. I had not dug deeply enough to see that though Blacks suffer the time and space subjugation of cartographic deracination and the hydraulics of the capitalist working day, we also suffer as the hosts of Human parasites, though they themselves might be the hosts of parasitic capital and colonialism. I had looked to the humanities (first as a creative practitioner and critical theorist) to help me find/create the story of Black liberation—Black political redemption. What I found instead was that redemption *as a genre* was a parasite that fed on me for its coherence. Everything meaningful in my life had been housed under the umbrellas called "the humanities" and "radical politics." The parasites had been capital, colonialism, patriarchy, homophobia. And now it was clear that I had missed the boat. My parasites were Humans, all Humans—the haves as well as the have-nots. If the disciplines that compose the humanities and radical politics are to rid themselves of the parasitism that they heretofore have had in common with radical and progressive movements on the Left—that is, if our disciplinary labors are to face, rather than disavow, the discrepancy between *Humans* who suffer through an "economy of disposability"[5] and *Blacks* who suffer by way of "social death"[6]—then we must come to grips with how the redemption of the subaltern (a narrative, for example, of Palestinian *plenitude, loss*, and *restoration*) is made possible by the (re)instantiation of a regime of violence that bars Black people from the imaginary of redemption.

Nabil and I didn't share a universal, postcolonial grammar of suffering. Nabil's loss is tangible: land. When it is not tangible, it is at least coherent: the loss of labor power. The paradigm of *his* dispossession elaborates capitalism and the colony. But how does one describe the loss that makes the world if all that can be said of loss is locked within the world? In other words, how does one narrate absence, the loss of loss? Baldwin came close when he tried to explain why his friendship with Mailer ended: the "difference between . . . something to save . . . [and nothing] to lose."[7] Nabil forced me to face the depth of isolation in ways I had wanted to avoid—a deep pit from which neither postcolonial theory, nor Marxism, nor the radical gender politics of unflinching feminism could rescue me.

What is striking for me about this vignette is the ease with which the concrete reality of Black people is rendered in metaphoric terms. The vignette illustrates what Jared Sexton calls the "hidden structure of violence that underwrites so many violent acts, whether spectacular or mundane."[8] This metaphoric appropriation of social death as a means of coming to grips with the violence of social life is the result of a special kind of imaginative labor, one in which Blackness functions as a spectacle for the production of optimism (or pessimism) with respect to the structural oppression of all sorts of people who are not Black. We see this in immigration discourse (Muslims are the "new niggers"). The Black imago functions on several levels here: as the destination of civil society's libidinal aggression and as the target of its relentless prelogical rituals of violence. Whereas the Human's relationship to violence is always contingent, triggered by her transgressions against the regulatory prohibitions of the Symbolic Order or by macroeconomic shifts in her social context, the Slave's relationship to violence is open-ended, gratuitous, without reason or constraint, triggered by prelogical catalysts that are unmoored from her transgressions and unaccountable to historical shifts. In short, the violence inflicted upon Black people is not the effect of symbolic transgressions, nor is it the result (as Allen Feldman would have it[9]) of a new, global shift in political economy—it is an extension of the master's prerogative. Orlando Patterson clarifies this distinction between violence that positions and punishes the Human (worker, postcolonial subject, woman, or queer, for example) and violence that positions and punishes the Slave (the Black) by emphasizing the difference between the violence that constitutes capitalism and the violence that constitutes slavery. The worker who is fired remains a worker, to be hired elsewhere. The slave who was freed was no longer a slave. Thus it was necessary continually to repeat the original, violent act of transforming free man into slave. This act of violence constitutes the prehistory of all stratified societies, but it determines both "the prehistory and (concurrent) history of slavery."[10] After 9/11 we saw how a vast number of Muslim civil rights activists referenced themselves as the "new niggers." Blackness (or "nigger") labors as a signifier beneath which the signified does not slide, as if to say "our white experience or our Muslim experience of violence becomes real when likened to a figure (the Black) whose experience with violence is *of the Real*"—that is to say, violence beyond signification. But a Black person could not process her loss or grief at the death of Sandra Bland by drawing on white or Muslim death. *It's happening to us like it's happening to them* is not a signified that can slide under the signifier Black.

Empathy is a kind of violence: identification based upon the projection of oneself into the suffering of another. This is clear from the research of psychoanalytic thinkers like Kaja Silverman. I am not disputing this, nor am I suggesting that there is an empathic paradigm that operates, schematically, through strategies that do not facilitate identification via projection and, ultimately, captation of the Other.[11] What I am arguing is that the modality of reciprocity is embedded in this transaction. And it is this modality, reciprocity, that *can* give reciprocity its ethical dimension. Blacks, however, are structurally barred from the modality of reciprocity. And it is this injunction, instantiated ab initio, that is the problem: the slave is an instrument and implement of empathy, not an agent of empathy.[12] The structure of violence that elaborates and positions the Black is ontologically irreconcilable with the structure of violence that subjugates the Human.

To illustrate what I mean, I offer my poem "Law Abiding." Returning to and explicating this poem helps to clarify how the regime of violence that saturates Blacks is structurally incompatible with a regime of violence where contingency, as opposed to saturation, is the operative modality, and how this regime of violence comes with touchstones of cohesion necessary for redemption.

Law Abiding

For Oscar Grant

Don't slant the story to fit your needs
Bullets been catching hell from niggers long as I been born
Like apples ok you got your few bad bullets
But most work hard and vote yes they vote and
Got wives and sweet kids in the clip
Who cradles them when a nigger vamps who says
What to them
Mrs. Bullet I have some bad news
Then what
It's about your husband Mr. John Fredrick Bullet
Or
May I call you Frieda
Frieda John Fredrick passed this evening
Now Frieda be strong for unsavory
Are the details
He died in a nigger's spine
Crushed on impact now Frieda don't cry
The D.A.'s on it
The judge's been briefed
And your husband's friends are
In the streets[13]

At first blush an exegesis might be seduced into emphasizing what this poem has in common with a U.S. liberal order that promises an eventual end to racism and the happy universalism to follow. But the poem actually shows that other kinds of endemic violence—against Native Americans, for example—are not analogous to the violence by which Blacks are elaborated and positioned. The violence of social death (that violence which elaborates and reproduces the slave) is fundamentally different from the violence that usurps American land or attempts to destroy the Indian's cultural and territorial sovereignty. A poem about the latter, for example, Simon Ortiz's epic poem *Sand Creek*, takes the relational status of both the Indian victims and the white oppressors as established—a reciprocal dynamic is acknowledged (between degraded humanity, Indians, and exalted humanity, white settlers).[14]

This reciprocal dynamic is based on the fact that even though one group is massacring the other, both exist within the same paradigm of recognition and incorporation. Their relation is based on a *mutual* recognition of sovereignty. At every scale of abstraction—body, family, community, cosmology, physical terrain—Native American sovereignty is recognized and incorporated into the consciousness of both Indians and the settlers who destroyed them. Such a poem's coherence is sustained by structural capacity for reciprocity between the genociders and the genocided. This structural reciprocity presents a vision of hope amid the violence, manifested in a sense of spatial presence (images of land and weather) and in the sense that for both groups, a future is possible. This means that the violence the Indians suffer has a utility (confiscation and occupation of land) that makes it legible and coherent.

The future belongs to the bullet. Filiation belongs to the bullet. Our caring energies will be reserved not for the Black but for the bullet. Reciprocity is not a constituent element of the struggle between beings who are socially dead and those who are socially alive—the struggle between Blacks and the world.

We need to apprehend the profound and irreconcilable difference between white supremacy (the *colonial utility* of settlement) and anti-Blackness (the human race's *necessity* for violence against Black people). The antagonism between the postcolonial subject and the settler (the Sand Creek massacre or the Palestinian Nakba) cannot—and should not be—analogized with the violence of social death: that is the violence of slavery, which did not end in 1865, for the simple reason that slavery did not end in 1865. Slavery is a relational dynamic just as colonialism is a relational dynamic—not an event and certainly not a place in space like the South—and that relational dynamic can continue to exist once the settler has left or ceded governmental power. And these two relations are secured by radically different structures of violence. Afro-pessimism offers an analytic lens that labors as a corrective to humanist assumptive logic. It provides a theoretical apparatus that allows Black people to *not* have to be burdened by the ruse of analogy—because analogy *mystifies*, rather than clarifies, Black suffering. Analogy mystifies Black people's relationship to other people of color. Afro-pessimism labors to throw this mystification into relief—without fear of the fault lines and fissures that emerge in the process.

There is a compulsive and repetitive "failure" in the poem titled "Law Abiding," as though, in writing the poem, I unconsciously realized the futility of asserting something within Blackness that is prior to the devastation that defines Blackness; and the force of the repetition compulsion with which the poem roils within this devastation is vertiginous. "The D.A.'s on it / The judge has been briefed / And your husband's friends are / In the streets[.]"

The poem contains no lines, no fragments, that can be cobbled together with enough muscle to check this devastation, to act on it in a contrapuntal way. This is not a case of the "compulsion to repeat," which Freud describes in *Beyond the Pleasure Principle*, whereby the repetition is "something that seems . . . more elementary, more instinctual than the pleasure principle which it overrides."[15] "Law Abiding" contains no political strategy or therapeutic agency through which the violence that engulfs Black flesh can be separated from the poem's compulsion to repeat that violence.

In a "normal" situation—that is to say, if "Law Abiding" was a poem about human trauma and genocide—therapeutic and/or political intervention could be made, in the case of therapy, to help the poet become aware of a distinction between the violence he may indeed encounter from the state and a range of psychic alternatives to letting that violence consume his unconscious; and, in the case of politics, the vision elaborated by a movement could help the poet imagine a new day, and thus imbue state violence with a temporal finitude ("our day will come," as the Irish Republican Army used to say, and so it did; or the Native American dream of Turtle Island *restored*; or the end of Israeli occupation) even if the poet didn't live to experience that finitude. But recourse to political and therapeutic resources presumes a potential for separating skeins of unconscious compulsion (the poem's repetitive compulsion) from the violence whose incursions are being compulsively repeated. This presumption only works for human subjects, subjects whose relationship to violence is contingent on their transgressions. The slave's relationship to violence is not contingent; it is gratuitous—it bleeds out beyond the grasp of narration, from the Symbolic to the Real, where therapy and politics have no purchase.

Neither filial conflict (to be resolved, for example, through therapy) nor affilial conflict (to be resolved through politics and insurgent resistance) has purchase in a struggle for Black redemption.[16] With the lines "Mrs. Bullet I have some bad news . . . It's about your husband Mr. John Fredrick Bullet / Or / May I call you Frieda," the poem seems to realize that the integrity of gender is more properly the possession of an inanimate *bullet* than of a sentient Black being. The violence against Black people we are witnessing on YouTube videos, on Instagram, and on television news is conveniently gendered as violence against Black men. But there is a problem here, and it is twofold: we tend to lose sight of the fact that Black women, children, and LGBT people are losing their breath through the technologies of social death, just as Black hetero men are, albeit in less visible and less mediatized ways; we also get drawn into responding to the phobic anxieties of white and non-Black civil society, the threat of the Black man, and as such we offer sustenance to that juggernaut (civil society) even as we try to dismantle it. We enhance the pleasurable circulation of the modern lynching photograph (i.e., the cover of *Time* magazine with a still image from the video taken April 4, 2015, showing a North Charleston, South Carolina, policeman shooting Walter Scott in the back as he runs away) and the snuff videos (of, for example, Sandra Bland's and Eric Garner's police encounters) on which Black political organizers have come to depend to *show* the world police violence in an effort, ironically, to redress that violence. And, since these images are almost always of Black males, they shape our (Black humanist) agenda in profoundly gendered ways. But there is something even more problematic: we come to think of our oppression as being *essentially* gendered, as opposed to being gendered in important ways. This, I believe, gives us a false sense of agency, a sense that we can redress the violence of social death in ways analogous to the tactics of our so-called allies of color. We *want* the violence against us to have a gendered integrity, in the way that it does when it is levied against the subaltern. But gender is scandalized (not merely *for* but) by the slave.

The following example from popular culture illustrates what I am trying to say about how gender is scandalized when interrogated through the interpretive lens of the Black—the slave. There's a cable television series, called *Homeland*, about the trials and tribulations of a CIA officer named Carrie Mathison. In one episode, her cover is that of an investigative journalist, who convinces the nephew of an Afghan Taliban leader that she can get him out of Islamabad and help him find safe haven in England.[17] She convinces him that the two of them must stay holed up in a secret apartment for three days as transport is being arranged for his safe passage. It's all a lie. She's really using him as bait to lure his uncle into a trap so that she might assassinate him. In point of fact, the apartment is a CIA safe house in which Carrie holds this young man captive. She then proceeds to seduce him. He thinks they are in the throes of some sort of love affair that is overdetermined by mutual consent. In other words, he doesn't know that he is being raped, repeatedly—that his consent to this sex has been abrogated by the very structure of the conditions in which the sex takes place. It is a rape scenario because the sex that he mistakes for mutual attraction is really a series of multiple acts of aggression in which his consent has been eviscerated, completely. The gun the white woman holds to his head needn't be in her hand. In fact, the gun she holds to his head is not one weapon but the weapons of three million soldiers in uniform and their arsenal of drones and technologies of death. She forces sex upon him through her capacity—the capacity that her white skin embodies. Another way of saying this is to say that white desire is always already weaponized. She forces sex on him through the capacity that white bodies have to weaponize white desire. The young Afghan man is fucked! He is fucked at every level of abstraction. The guns are in the bedroom (Carrie Mathison's hidden pistol). The guns are also pointed at his head from outside in the street: the CIA operatives who watch the house. And the guns are held to his head from high above, in the nine thousand drones that saturate the sky and track him as he makes his way back to Carrie's genuine objective—his uncle, the Taliban leader whom she hopes to murder at long range.

We have here a pristine example of the ways in which white femininity *and* white masculinity occupy the same *structural* position in relation to a man or a woman of color. To paraphrase Frantz Fanon, the white family is the cutout of the state.[18] Jared Sexton puts a finer point on this dynamic. In so doing, he is careful not to include the Afghan young man being raped by a white woman, as I have, but to home in on the specificity of the Black. Sexton writes,

> [It] seems counterintuitive . . . [but] because of her historical implication in the structures of white supremacy (marked by her limited *capacity to marshal* state violence or state sanctioned paramilitary violence), the white woman can have the black man (or black woman) brutalized for transgressions real or imagined. However, and because of this relation of power, *she can also rape him,* thereby *reversing the polarity of a rape fantasy* pervasive in the anti-black world; regardless of his size and strength, his prowess and his pride, he is *structurally vulnerable* to her. (Contrary to many standard legal definitions, she is able to rape him without his necessarily being physically penetrated against his will. In this sense, the fear of rape and the fear of penetration must be *carefully distinguished.*) Perhaps rape is better understood not as an isolated act, but as part of *a spectrum of sexual coercion generated within a broader set of social, political, and economic relations* regulated (but not simply controlled) by the racial state and enabling permutations of enactment.[19]

Saidiya Hartman's diachronic explanation of the paradigm of anti-Black sexual violation concurs with Sexton's synchronic explanation of the paradigm: in the nineteenth century, "enslaved men were no less vulnerable to the wanton abuses of their owners, although the extent of their sexual exploitation will probably never be known, and because of the elusiveness or instability of gender in relation to the slave as property and the erotics of terror in the racist imaginary."[20]

And we can see how the geopolitical agendas of the white nation cannot be disentangled from the sex life of white femininity and white masculinity. White sexuality is always already weaponized. To put it differently, but no less to the point, the United States of America is a big, bad rapist—a big, bad rapist that *projects* the fantasy of *its* vulnerability onto Muslims, Mexicans, Native Americans, and Blacks. Fanon discusses the rape fantasy of the white woman in great detail in *Black Skin, White Masks*. I won't rehearse it here. For our purposes we should note that the rapist projects the fantasy of vulnerability by suggesting that she or he is the victim of Islamic jihadism or the victim of Black agitation against cop killing. The big, bad rapist would have us believe that *America* is the victim and that underneath that phantasmagoric projection, underneath the fantasy of vulnerability, is a set of assumptions that America is indeed an ethical social and political formation, that the problems that America has are *not* structural but rather performative (i.e., to be found in acts of discrimination or in the use of excessive levels of force). What I am interested in here, however, is not a *moral* rejoinder to acts of sexual violation but an *ethical* analysis of the structure of violence that subtends this fantasy—the institutional violence that gives these fantasies what David Marriott calls "objective value."[21] Jared Sexton gives us a concrete explanation of Marriott's phrase "objective value" when he says, "You'd better understand White people's fantasies because tomorrow they'll be legislation."[22] That's what the law is: the white fantasy as objective value.

The white family and the white state have the firepower and the institutional infrastructure to enforce their projections. What people of color get to do when they go to the polls is decide what flavor of this rape fantasy they are going to support. In the words of George Jackson, "an electoral choice of ten different fascists is like choosing which way one wishes to die." We have to dig deeper and see how the structure of and capacity for world making is predicated on sexualized violence against Black people. Sexualized violence against Black people is politics' very *condition of possibility*.

Anti-Blackness is the genome of electoral politics. In short, anti-Blackness is the genetic material of this organism called the United States of America. The fantasy projections that have been weaponized to rape the young Afghan man would not be possible if the paradigm of the weaponization were not already in place prior to the conflict between Muslims and the United States—and that weaponized paradigm is overdetermined by anti-Blackness. The U.S. government *could* become a democracy for people of color who are not Black (it's not likely, but it is entirely possible); but if it ever rid itself of the central ingredient that overdetermines its condition of possibility—that is to say, if the United States of America were to somehow not be anti-Black—then we would no longer have a country; the United States of America would cease to exist.

I've explained how the United States is an anti-Black polity by using a synchronic analysis of domesticity. Now, I want to examine how it is also *historically* unethical: how the United States is diachronically anti-Black. A recent history book does this brilliantly: *The American Slave Coast: A History of the Slave-Breeding Industry* by Ned and Constance Sublette. A small portion of the book focuses on the electoral college. The electoral college is a prime example of a so-called democratic institution that owes its *condition of possibility* to the sexualized violence against and captivity of Black people.[23] Without the sexualized violence against and mass incarceration of hundreds of thousands of Black captives, Americans would not be able to elect a president. Thomas Jefferson would never have become president. In the late eighteenth and early nineteenth centuries, "389,000 [that's fewer than half a million] . . . African slaves, bred like horses or sheep, became four million enslaved African-Americans. . . . The forced mating of slaves . . . gave slave states more voting power based on the number of slaves they held captive."[24] Virginia was the largest slave-breeding state; as a result, it gained 25 percent of the forty-six electoral college votes—more than enough to send Jefferson to the White House.

Let us stop and think about that for a moment. Slave breeding is a form of captivity, the scale of which dwarfs the kind of captivity to which Muslims are subjected in Guantánamo or in the "love nest" where the female CIA agent raped the young Afghan. How else can 389,000 people be made to procreate, under pain of torture or death, into four million people if they are not incarcerated and forced into sex? Slave breeding is a kind of forced sex that makes words like *rape* and *incarceration* puny and inadequate. The young Afghan man had a prior moment of freedom, and a prior space of consent, before the white women held him captive and raped him. For Blacks, there is no prior space and time of freedom and consent: the freedom of all others—in the form of electoral politics—owes its condition of possibility to the unfreedom (lack of consent) and sexualized violence against Black people. People of color *experience this madness from time to time*, but the forced procreation of Blackness is the bedrock of this madness.

The young Afghan's rights were violated by the white woman, but the *concept* of rights that can be violated, or respected, rises up out of the breeding of Blacks like cattle. You can speak of prisoners' rights, but the term *slave rights* is an oxymoron. A diachronic analysis of the electoral college, much like a synchronic analysis of the vignette from Berkeley or *Homeland*, illustrates how Black people are political *currency*, not political *subjects*. And that is the paradigm of Black people's existence today. Black people are political currency or objects, not political actors or subjects. Subjects have homes, or at least the capacity for some sort of sanctuary. Objects exist as implements in the psychic dwellings of subjects.

Notes

1. David Marriott, *On Black Men* (New York: Columbia University Press, 2000); David Marriott, *Haunted Life: Visual Culture and Black Modernity* (New Brunswick, N.J.: Rutgers University Press, 2007).
2. Marriott, *On Black Men*.
3. Frantz Fanon, *Black Skin, White Masks*, trans. Constance Farrington (New York: Grove, 1967), 146.
4. Saidiya Hartman, *Scenes of Subjection: Terror, Slavery, and Self-Making in Nineteenth-Century America* (Oxford: Oxford University Press, 1997), 65.
5. Jared Sexton, "Afro-Pessimism: The Unclear Word," *Rhizomes: Cultural Studies in Emerging Knowledge*, no. 29 (2016), https://doi.org/10.20415/rhiz/029.e02.
6. Orlando Patterson, *Slavery and Social Death: A Comparative Study* (Cambridge, Mass.: Harvard University Press, 1982).
7. James Baldwin, *Nobody Knows My Name: More Notes of a Native Son* (New York: Dial Press, 1961), 172.
8. Sexton, "Afro-Pessimism."
9. Allen Feldman, *Formations of Violence: The Narrative of the Body and Political Terror in Northern Ireland* (Chicago: University of Chicago Press, 1991).

10. Patterson, *Slavery and Social Death*, 3.
11. Kaja Silverman, *Male Subjectivity at the Margins* (New York: Routledge, 1992).
12. Hartman, *Scenes of Subjection*.
13. Frank B. Wilderson III, “Law Abiding,” in *Stand Our Ground: Poems for Trayvon Martin and Marissa Alexander*, ed. Ewuare X. Osayande (Philadelphia: Freedom Seed Press, 2013).
14. Simon J. Ortiz, *From Sand Creek* (Tucson: University of Arizona Press, 1981). The Sand Creek massacre took place on November 29, 1864. A winter encampment of Arapaho and Cheyenne had settled near Sand Creek in southeastern Colorado Territory when a 675-man force of Colorado U.S. Volunteer Cavalry attacked the encampment, killing and mutilating an estimated 230 Native Americans, more than half of them women and children. The location is now a historic site administered by the National Park Service. National Park Service, “Sand Creek Massacre,” last updated March 3, 2017, https://www.nps.gov/sand/learn/historyculture/massacre.htm.
15. Sigmund Freud, *Beyond the Pleasure Principle* (Cambridge: Cambridge University Press, 1920), 23.
16. *Filial*: any community into which one is born—nation, religion, ethnicity, family. *Affilial*: a voluntary association, a community one chooses to enter. In *The World, the Text, and the Critic*, Edward Said describes affiliation as “the transition from a failed idea or possibility of filiation to a kind of compensatory order that, whether it is a party, an institution, a culture, a set of beliefs, or even a world-vision, provides men and women with a new form of relationship, which I have been calling affiliation but which is also a new system. Now whether we look at this new affiliative mode of relationship as it is to be found among conservative writers like Eliot or among progressive writers like Lukacs and, in his own special way, Freud, we will find the deliberately explicit goal of using that new order to reinstate vestiges of the kind of authority associated in the past with filiative order. This, finally, is the third part of the pattern. Freud’s psychoanalytic guild and Lukacs’ notion of the vanguard party are no less providers of what we might call a restored authority. The new hierarchy or, if it is less a hierarchy than a community, the new community is greater than the individual adherent or member, just as the father is greater by virtue of seniority than the sons and daughters; the ideas, values, and the systematic totalizing world-view validated by the new af-

filiative order are all bearers of authority too, with the result that something resembling a cultural system is established. Thus if a filial relationship was held together by natural bonds and natural forms of authority—involving obedience, fear, love, respect, and instinctual conflict—the new affiliative relationship changes these bonds into what seem to be transpersonal forms [for our purposes, mediating objects]—such as guild consciousness, consensus, collegiality, professional respect, class and the hegemony of a dominant culture. The filiative scheme belongs to the realms of nature and of 'life,' whereas affiliation belongs exclusively to culture and society." Said, *The World, the Text, and the Critic* (Cambridge, Mass.: Harvard University Press, 1984), 19–20.

17. *Homeland*, season 4, episode 5, "About a Boy," directed by Charlotte Sieling, aired October 26, 2014, on HBO.
18. The paraphrase comes from *Black Skin, White Masks* in the chapter titled "The Negro and Psychopathology." In espionage parlance, a cutout is a mutually trusted intermediary, method, or channel of communication that facilitates the exchange of information between agents. Cutouts usually know only the source and destination of the information to be transmitted, not the identities of any other persons involved in the espionage process (a need-to-know basis). Thus a captured cutout cannot be used to identify members of an espionage cell.
19. Jared Sexton, "Race, Sexuality, and Political Struggle: Reading 'Soul on Ice,'" *Social Justice* 30, no. 2 (2003): 28–41. Emphasis added.
20. Hartman, *Scenes of Subjection*, 81.
21. See his book *On Black Men*.
22. From a workshop Sexton conducted for Black undergraduate student organizers at the University of California, Berkeley in 2000.
23. Ned and Constance Sublette, *The American Slave Coast: A History of the Slave-Breeding Industry* (Chicago: Chicago Review Press, 2015).
24. Lee Ballinger, "The Review of *The American Slave Coast: A History of the Slave-Breeding Industry*," *CounterPunch* 22, no. 10 (2016).

6

Afro-Pessimism and Non-Philosophy at the Zero Point of Subjectivity, History, and Aesthetics

Andrew Culp

How to think today? Poststructuralism is in obvious decline. It has been met, on one hand, by a resurgent identity politics and, on the other, by a very different turn toward realism. An exemplar of the former is Afro-pessimism, that thought that takes the gratuitous violence used to conserve the structural positionality of the slave as constituting the anti-Black world, of the latter, the non-philosophy of François Laruelle, which accuses philosophy of cheating thought by claiming to investigate notions before, above, or otherwise outside reality. At first blush, one might question whether the militant Blackness of Afro-pessimism and the winding thought of nonstandard philosophy should even be discussed in the same breath. This observation is especially relevant, as both are careful players in the great game of the politics of association.

Methodologically, Afro-pessimism proceeds by way of an "unflinching paradigmatic analysis" of the structure of anti-Black violence.[1] The affective tonality in how it names its method is important. In its steadfastness, Afro-pessimism stands against the easy move toward solutions. Certainly the search for solutions treats problems as something to resolve quickly rather than sitting with what makes so many of them intractable. And as Nahum Chandler has argued, academics are especially eager to jump beyond concepts associated with race rather than treat it as an ongoing reality that makes up the world.[2] In contrast, Afro-pessimism boldly responds to the question ("How does it feel to be a problem?") that routinely rendered W. E. B. Du Bois silent—paving a path not toward the liberation of Blackness from being a problem but imagining all being as a problem of Blackness. As such, Afro-pessimism turns away from poststructuralism's emphasis on subjective capacity, historical transformation through the contingency of violence, and intersectional theories of identity. As a rough guide, Frank B. Wilderson III thus suggests that those engaging its conceptual problematics ask themselves, "Am I engaging with [Afro-pessimism] to understand and explain more deeply the condition of Black subjugation; or am I engaging with this theory to figure out which aspects of it I can pinch for myself and my points of attention that have nothing to do with Black suffering?"[3] Such concerns are only magnified by Selamawit Terrefe and Christina Sharpe, who are deeply troubled by "white male academics of a certain age group" who seem "excited" by Afro-pessimism's meditation on Black suffering to the point of being *invigorated* by it as "a purely intellectual enterprise."[4]

Using a parallel set of criticisms, François Laruelle might appear as just another in the long string of post–World War II French thinkers who have so often been an obstacle for Black studies. At the level of style, Laruelle's nonstandard philosophy would seem to confirm this unfavorable assessment—it works by way of axiomatic inquiry familiar to the geometric reason of French rationalism and claims to uphold its own version of science. Concepts central to nonstandard philosophy's project of radical immanence (the One, the philosophical decision, the real) do not appear immediately relevant to a structural understanding of Black suffering. In fact, French philosophical writing on Blackness often rushes to overcome the question of race by declaring it as an error of thought, as in Alain Badiou's recent *Black: The Brilliance of a Non-Color*. Given these tendencies, it is just as likely that Afro-pessimism and nonstandard philosophy are primed for a nonencounter, like ships passing in the night, two impermeable vessels deep into their own voyages.

However, a small body of scholarship has connected the two

areas of thought. From one direction, scholars have examined how Laruelle's thought contributes to Blackness. Tavia Nyong'o, Eugene Thacker, Aria Dean, the Otolith Group, Ariane Queneau, and others have examined this, largely through readings of his essay "On the Black Universe: In the Human Foundations of Color." It is common for these readings ultimately to diverge from Afro-pessimism through a vitalist reading of Laruelle's text. From another direction, a bridge has been built by scholars of non-philosophy, such as Anthony Paul Smith and Daniel Colucciello Barber. Smith establishes the parallels between the two figures of Laruelle's stranger and Afro-pessimism's slave, whose deracinating rootlessness threatens to tear apart the world from the inside.[5] My argument is that the encounter between the two projects is due to a co-incidence, a shared approach to the time of an event. What event? A turning away from poststructuralist philosophy. Their departure is not just with a specific brand of philosophy but an escape from standard philosophical procedures. Each in its own way, the projects mark the exhaustion of the cultural politics of difference, namely, the tactical politics of historical contingency, subjectivity-centered models of coalition building, and psychoanalytic theories of liberation.

Taking this insight seriously leads to three interrelated concepts on which other scholars have built the coincidence between Afro-pessimism and nonstandard philosophy: the politics of withdrawal, non-philosophical theories of Blackness as ontological death, and the determinate uchromia of the world. It would be tempting simply to chart how these concepts communicate across two very different intellectual projects, showing how each elaborates on elements of the other. Yet communication in its purest form is not the transfer of meaning; it is contamination—so while previous scholars have only forged the connection, it proves more critical to describe how these concepts shape, amend, and transform theories central to Afro-pessimism and nonstandard philosophy. This is also why each section begins with a vignette, neither to factualize Blackness, to circulate spectacular images of anti-Black violence, nor to materialize the suffering of Black bodies as objects to be repossessed through white empathy. Rather, by providing the bruising prick of a *punctum*, they draw the reader away from treating Blackness as just another abstract currency for white speculation.

Withdrawal: Nonsubjectivity

> The Zong massacre provides a paradigmatic case for the status of blackness. The Zong, a ship named after the Dutch word for care, was a slave ship used in the triangle trade. Its owners became mired in a legal dispute stemming from the crew's decision to throw over a hundred of their slaves overboard. In their estimate, if crew were able to prove to their insurers that their decision was justified in the name of saving the rest of the "cargo," they could also collect insurance on dead slaves otherwise not covered in the event of "natural death" at sea. The insurer's lawyers preached about human rights and racial equality, knowing full well that the crew was not facing accusations of murder and instead choosing humanism as the best cover to avoid an insurance payout. In fact, when criminal charges were suggested for the captain and his crew, Solicitor-General John Lee is said to have responded by saying, "What is this claim that human people have been thrown overboard? This is a case of chattels or goods. Blacks are goods and property; it is madness to accuse these well-serving honourable men of murder. They acted out of necessity and in the most appropriate manner for the cause. . . . To question the judgement of an experienced, well-traveled captain held in the highest regard is one of folly, especially when talking of slaves. The case is the same as if horses had been thrown overboard."[6]

Afro-pessimism and nonstandard philosophy both begin with a turning away from studying the human as empirical object.[7] An important realization of this move is each project's withdrawal from Marxist notions of the subject. On this account, Wilderson provides a clear account, in that he finds Marxism unsuitable for "(a) describing the structure of antagonism, (b) delineating the proper revolutionary subject, and (c) elaborating a trajectory of institutional iconoclasm comprehensive enough to start 'the only thing in the world that's worth the effort of starting: the end of the world, by God!' "[8] Although he chooses to sidestep an antagonistic relationship to Marxism, Laruelle's own "non-Marxist" subject is set on similarly heretical path against the (empirical) world.[9]

This allows Afro-pessimism to depart from a Marxist theory of the subject, supplanting it with Blackness as defined by social death. The term *social death* originates with Orlando Patterson, whose study of enslavement and social death outlines three characteristics: natal alienation, general dishonor, and naked/gratuitous violence.[10] Its importance is clear when considering how "radicalized" paradigms like gentrification and carceral capitalism do not follow from older categories of political economy. Even in a world of carceral capitalism, surplus value extraction provides little to explain the gratuitous violence associated with the summary executions of Trayvon Martin, Michael Brown, and Atatiana Jefferson.

Consider how Afro-pessimists read Frantz Fanon's *Black Skin, White Masks,* which is largely considered a phenomenological text about interrelation—especially when authors refer to the more faithful translation of the chapter on the hail, "The Lived Experience of the Black Man."[11] Afro-pessimists do not read it for its rendering of the experience of the Black man; they read Fanon for the structural positionality of Blackness. This reading diverges from Fanon's use of Jean-Paul Sartre, who argues that race holds no fixed content because it is the anti-Semite who creates the Jew: "If the Jew did not exist, the anti-Semite would invent him."[12]

Afro-pessimism withdraws from relations altogether—those of coloniality, white supremacy, and other intersubjective theories of Blackness. As Jared Sexton argues, "the color line, as it were, operates here as the division of the world into regions of blackness and non-blackness, or slavery contrasted to forms of freedom including the possessive investment in whiteness, rather than whiteness and non-whiteness, or freedom as the possessive investment in whiteness contrasted with forms of unfreedom defined by its relative absence or prohibition."[13] It is a political ontology that thinks the concept of Blackness on its own terms. Immanently. Something sprung forth in the hold of the slave ships as they crossed the Atlantic. And in turn, asserting the absence of Black subjectivity (and homeland, and political sovereignty) that can never be fully realized, Afro-pessimism takes leave of Black consciousness, vitalist, and other liberationist theories.[14] As such, Afro-pessimism trades historical contingency for the consistency of the paradigm. It is here that we see the immanence of Laruelle overlap with the unflinching paradigmatic analysis of Blackness.

Black social death operates within its own libidinal economy in which death is used as psychic currency for nonslaves.[15] This is not a position specific to Afro-pessimism, having emerged as a critical theme in the Black study of race and gender. For example, the particular structural positioning of "(white) culture's dependence on the nonhuman status of its black subjects" as it rests on "the status of the black as a nonentity" is explored by Sharon P. Holland in her ongoing work on the libidinal economy, though her focus is often on the psychic structures and experiences of subjectivity.[16] Moreover, Hortense Spillers remains the canonical reference for the consumption of Black bodies as fungible objects, and of how the trauma of the Middle Passage has created a grammar of suffering that cannot be spoken, and that the Black woman serves as "the principal point of passage between the human and the non-human world."[17]

The social withdrawal of social death as such a defining characteristic of Afro-pessimism parallels aspects of Laruelle's thought. Specifically, Laruelle begins with an immanence that abstains from the philosophical decision and thus a nonparticipation in relations. He plays in reverse the concept of Derridean withdrawal, which provoked a debate between Philippe Lacoue-Labarthe and Jean-Luc Nancy on "the withdraw/retreat [*retrait*] of the political." Borrowing Claude Lefort's distinction between politics and the political, they argued that the authority on which political power is granted is now fully taken for granted by politics—that juridical frameworks, such as civil, political, and human rights, appear as the only way that politics is done. As Nancy says, such formal abstraction "undoubtedly 'does right' by every participatory and every relation, but without giving this right any meaning other than itself."[18] The consequence is a version of Debord's society of the spectacle whereby the political is subsumed into "a self-representation that no longer refers to an origin, but only to the void of its own specularity."[19] Even given this as a convincing diagnosis, Lacoue-Labarthe and Nancy provide a dissatisfying turn to philosophical reflection by proposing a return to "the *philosophical* questioning of the political" and "the questioning of the philosophical *about* the political."[20]

Laruelle's abolition of the philosophical decision strikes against the entire phenomenological tradition. He does not imagine that there are subjective experiences or subject–object relations that hide behind the curtain of thought. Such transcendental logic is philosophy's "oldest prejudice": the correlationist's determination that behind the world lies a secret set of conditions that can be found.[21] As Alexander R. Galloway has argued, Laruelle's general approach is to eliminate relational thinking altogether.[22]

Following the task outlined by Sabine Broeck—"to programmatically disrupt and limit, as far as possible, the workings of humanism, and its ongoing anti-Blackness"—Anthony Paul Smith and Daniel Colucciello Barber have each worked to undermine the whiteness that constitutes philosophy.[23] The core of their work explores the overlap between Afro-pessimism with Laruelle's non-philosophy. It is worth noting that both have written significant treatments of Laruelle and immanence in religious thought, broadly speaking, Smith from the intersection of the religious and the ecological and Barber as an engagement with metaphysics. In recent years, each has a sustained engagement with Afro-pessimism in his work.

For Smith, the social death of the slave demonstrates the limits of philosophical thought, which has withheld the capacity of recognition from the enslaved to such a degree that philosophy does not even recognize the slave at all. Why else would the slave serve as a favored example for Enlightenment philosophers, whose position must always be held at a distance to ensure the possibility of freedom, reason, and civilization? Barber further considers the significance of Blackness as nonbeing, demonstrating how it problematizes philosophy's preferred methods of analogy, communication, possibility, and knowledge. The consequence for both is clear: the nonbeing of social death establishes *Blackness as the degree zero of subjectivity*. And as Laruelle argues in his theory of victimology, the way through is not to pity the nihilism of nonbeing in a move to redeem them; rather, the *non-* of *nonbeing* and its survival is an ultimatum that invites an insurrection against the world.[24]

Laruelle is challenged and challenging. On one hand, Laruelle deserves harsh criticism. Even when excoriating humanism, his analytic often resembles a motivating *aporia* not altogether different from Foucault's. Yet Laruelle's human is not underwritten by the same fairytale of plentitude of vitalist philosophies, whether of the monist-Spinozist or cosmopolitan-deconstructive variety. The central term to all of non-philosophy is the One. Its immanence informs Laruelle's ethical task of viewing "humanity" as indivisible and without recourse to essence or nature.[25] As such, Laruelle shares in Afro-pessimism's critique of the liberal subject as a fundamentally self-privileging project of stating "We are the World."[26] Non-philosophy takes the insufficiency of personhood as the generic condition of humanity. Said in other terms, Laruelle holds the withdrawal of subjectivity to be the cornerstone of all humanity.[27]

In an obverse move to the poststructuralists who continue to use a word—but under erasure—Laruelle maintains names like "humanity," but only after radically redefining them to no longer mean what they previously did. The risk is that a concept like "generic humanity" could be easily misread as a universal, virtually indistinguishable from the concept thoroughly exhausted by Marxists, cosmopolitans, and liberals. Afro-pessimism offers a striking clarification for how the generic should be thought as *subtraction*—the mechanism of subtraction beginning with Spillers's concept of pornotroping, whereby the Black body is stripped of personhood and made into flesh through violence and sexual objectification.[28]

More generally, Afro-pessimism and nonstandard philosophy share similarities to Giorgio Agamben's use of destituent power, a form of destitution that deactivates other powers that "never resolves itself into a constituted power."[29] As a wider range of thinkers has revealed, however, Agamben's philological investigations of destitution pale in comparison to Black study.[30] Moreover, it is essential to note that the term originated in Argentina around the 2001 crisis in which government after government resigned, fashioned by Colectivo Situaciones, who were undertaking research as they participated in unemployed people's *piquetes* road blockades.[31] One contemporary political working-out of this form of power is the Invisible Committee, whose book *Now* (2017) explores a "destituent process" that "calls for taking over the world and not taking power, for exploring new forms of life and not a new constitution, and for desertion and silence as alternatives to proclamations and crashes."[32] The trouble with these political projects is that they still seek to hold power, even if not in the constituted form that establishes sovereignty. From different sides, both nonstandard philosophy and Afro-pessimism insist against saving the world and instead suggest ways to end it.

In summary, Blackness is a "generic identity" in that it is absent of subjectivity, homeland, and political sovereignty.[33] What is lost is the loss of loss itself. Blackness here enters into the nonarchive of those lost *to* history: those whose presence never counted, whose absence was never accounted for, their existence unable to be recounted—that which does not even leave a trace.[34] The conventional response to such utter deracination usually turns to the Enlightenment project of growing human capacities through reason. Though as innumerable thinkers have shown, the triumph of reason is fundamentally anti-Black in its treatment of knowledge as a question of mastery over intellectual bondage.[35]

To the extent that Afro-pessimism demands a transformation in the state of affairs, which even thinkers like Calvin Warren question, it is not a return. The violence of anti-Blackness is not the result of alienation that could be resolved through measurable lumps of money or acres of land (though reparations or land reform would hardly hurt the cause). Echoing Laruelle's often-misread idea of the generic, Afro-pessimism offers Blackness as the degree zero of subjectivity. The "unbearable Blackness" of gratuitous violence, kinship eradication, cultural humiliation, erasure of homeland, and inaccessibility of political sovereignty is unique to the position of the slave. Yet, as a structural position, it is immanent to all bodies and identities. Generalizing Hortense Spillers's argument about the objectivization of the slave to the point of mere flesh, Afro-pessimism holds that Blackness exists paradigmatically at the "zero degree of social conceptualization"—the nonsubjective blackened structural position as a ground against which all subjectivity emerges.[36]

The starting point of nonsubjectivity cannot be with the struggle to fulfill universally the promises of self-possession, recognition, and community, then, but can only sit with the difficulty of

Jared Sexton's abolition declaration that "we are deracinated, and you can be too."[37] He expands on this notion elsewhere, explaining that

> a politics of abolition could never finally be a politics of resurgence, recovery, or recuperation. It could only ever begin with degeneration, decline, or dissolution. Abolition is the interminable radicalization of every radical movement, but a radicalization through the perverse affirmation of deracination, an uprooting of the natal, the nation, and the notion, preventing any order of determination from taking root, a politics without claim, without demand even, or a politics whose demand is "too radical to be formulated in advance of its deeds."[38]

Afro-pessimism marks the threshold of such generalized deracination through a concept Fanon borrows from his own mentor, Aimé Césaire, that "the only thing in the world that's worth starting: the end of the world."[39] Such a citational line stretches across a range of texts, from Frank B. Wilderson III's "Biko and the Problematic of Presence," " 'We Are Trying to Destroy the World': Anti-Blackness and Police Violence after Ferguson—An Interview with Frank B. Wilderson, III" by IMIXWHATILIKE, *Red, White, and Black: Cinema and the Structure of U.S. Antagonisms*, and "The Vengeance of Vertigo: Aphasia and Abjection in the Political Trials of Black Insurgents"; to Jared Sexton's " 'The Curtain of the Sky': An Introduction," "The Social Life of Social Death: On Afro-pessimism and Black Optimism," and "Unbearable Blackness"; to Jason R. Ambroise and Sabine Broeck's "Black Knowledges/Black Struggles: An Introduction"; to Calvin L. Warren's "Black Nihilism and the Politics of Hope," "Onticide: Afro-pessimism, ~~Gay~~ Nigger #1, and Surplus Violence," and *Ontological Terror: Blackness, Nihilism, and Emancipation*; to Sara-Maria Sorentino's "The Sociogeny of Social Death: Blackness, Modernity, and Its Metaphors in Orlando Patterson"; to M. Shadee Malaklou, "On the Chronopolitics of Black Social Life; or, How Mister Winfield 'Sends Go' "; to Eva Hayward and Che Gossett, "Impossibility of *That*," and so many more.[40]

The coincidence between the Afro-pessimist symbolic project to end the anti-Black world and non-philosophy's gnostic hatred of the world has not been lost on commentators. The parallels are noted by Anthony Paul Smith in chapters 5–7 of his *Laruelle: A Stranger to Thought* (2016) and by Daniel Colucciello Barber in "World-Making and Grammatical Impulse."[41] Although the coincidence has been forged into an immanent encounter through careful reading of Afro-pessimist texts, there remains a deep methodological question raised by Laruelle's theorization of heretics.[42] Death challenges the archive. Some murders allow the victims to live on as martyrs, rising out of ashes to form cinders in fiery phrases like "never again!" Other deaths do not simply consume bodies but burn them out of memory. Their disappearance is so complete that even their death is unrecoverable—unable to spark images of their suffering.[43] This raises a deathly serious question: how to remove whiteness from the politics of citationality, especially when Black suffering does not grant membership into a shared human condition but rather bears the mark of a deathly violence so gratuitous that it cannot even leave a fugitive trace?

The Paradigm: Noncontingency

With clockwork regularity, every four years, the U.S. electoral machine hits a fevered pitch. Black voters are the target of extra scrutiny and speculation. But unlike other voting blocks, no one asks *how* they will vote, just *if*. Why? "People tend to read black folks not voting as a sign of apathy, but, in fact, it is often an indication of a lack of faith in the political process that speaks to the conditions of the black community," has said Eddie Glaude.[44] Or as the headline of a recent op-ed for the website Afropunk states, "Black People Who Do Note Vote Are Not Stupid, and Many Vote Pushers Are Anti-Black."[45]

Significant structural forces are at play. There is a an almost irresistible urge to see the vote as an index of the potential for Black progress within liberal democracy. Whites have always worked to disenfranchise Black voters, overtly so through legal measures like literacy tests as well as voter ID laws and covertly through systemic disenfranchisement as well as intimidation. The reign of white terror exemplified by the hoods and burning crosses of the Klan was repeated in December 2016 as self-anointed "election monitors" showed up to polling stations with assault weapons. This display of force does not bear a directly causal relationship to Black voter turnout; rather, it points to the deeper channels of violence that uphold anti-Black civil society, explaining how Black absenteeism does not come from a place of apathy but as self-defense against a force working to "keep them in their place." This all goes to prove what Frank B. Wilderson III has argued, which is that in the eyes of voter-counters of every kind, "Black people are political currency, not political actors"—offering an explanation for why they vote despite it rarely serving their best interest.[46] In response, Calvin Warren suggests that the only reasonable solution is a Black nihilism, a Black political apostasy of self-excommunication from the body politic of the United States itself.[47]

Owing to its elucidatory pull, philosophy can be deadly for Blackness. After all, Fanon says that "philosophy never saved anybody."[48] In fact, he notes that philosophy's most virtuous aspirations are just as guilty for justifying "the extermination of men."[49] Better than doing philosophy, then, would be to embrace the non-philosophical project of "using philosophical materials to address non-philosophical questions." Afro-pessimism has already begun such an undertaking. As Jared Sexton has argued, "blackness is theory itself, anti-blackness the resistance to theory."[50]

In particular, Afro-pessimism may already signal a movement beyond the transcendental decision often found in historical inquiries. Post-Kantian transcendentalism speaks in a familiar voice of the truth of the subject. Perhaps the cornerstone to Laruelle's whole objection is captured in his essay "The Transcendental Method," in which he argues that "not every philosophy can be called transcendental, but the transcendental inheres in every philosophy."[51] The Afro-pessimist paradigmatic analysis is a method that refuses the transcendental "gesture." It dispenses with the philosophical adoption of the Kantian transcendental, which encourages poststructuralism's obsessive searches for transformations that begin from inside conceptions of the self. Further coinciding with Laruelle's turning away from the cryptic search for the thing-in-itself, Afro-pessimism begins from the starting that there is nothing cryptic or hidden about Black death that demands revelation. For, according to Wilderson, "the Black has no social relation(s) to be either masked or unmasked—not, that is, in a structural sense."[52]

The starkest conclusion of thinking Blackness "without-conditions" is that Blackness is then thought *as* captivity and not just *in* captivity, the latter formulation being latched on to by critics who misconstrue the project of Afro-pessimism. When those critics think captivity, their limited imaginations only apprehend Blackness as a subject in permanent arrested development—old tropes of a clever Blackness that tries to prove Black intelligence to no avail, a mutant Blackness that aspires to be white but always fails, or a Black liberation that sacrifices itself for others to recover value from being reduced to nothing. In conversation with Wilderson, Jaye Austin Williams clarifies this position by saying, "That's the *grave* misapprehension that people have about Afro-pessimism as a theoretical framing—that we're somehow against freedom; that we think black people are *inherently* slaves, incapacitated, and so on—when what they need to understand is that the lens of that critique is trained on the *world*, not on black people; *not* on their hopes for freedom or their desire to live and be alive."[53]

Thinking Blackness *as* captivity abolishes relation, replacing it with the radical immanence of the paradigm, which means no longer approaching it through historical theories of race (and their endless deferrals of its "true" cause, those always-debunked theories of hypodescent, phenotype, genetics, culture, and those yet to come).[54] The question of selfness and its impossibilities has already been raised by Hortense Spillers in her challenge to think "the concept of the 'one'"—perhaps the most important term to all of Laruelle's thought.[55] There are many possible directions to deepen this engagement, one already explored by Kevin Quashine, who theorizes a Black quietness through a oneness that "constitutes a sense of being capable of and related to everything."[56] Or as Sylvia Wynter argues, it means avoiding the code words for "genre."[57] Immanence gives Afro-pessimism the ability to think Blackness in the nonontology of enslavement, and nothing else.

Paradigmatically thinking of Blackness as immanence clarifies how to think three Laruellean moves: unilateralization, unidentification, and excarnation.[58]

Unilateral: Afro-pessimism thinks Blackness according to it being determined as nonbeing.

Unidentification: Afro-pessimism successfully accounts for the structural determination of Blackness as nonbeing, but with an attention to the way it is barred from investment in identity, such as social community, civil society, or certain categories (ethnicity, gender, ability status).[59]

Excarnation: Afro-pessimism's theorization of the persisting coincidence of Blackness and nonbeing as maintained in the real through identity (the trauma of *being* Black).

Thus Blackness remains the "position of the unthought" as long as identity (or subjective experience) remains the only resource for thought, yet in the Afro-pessimist treatment of Blackness through the unilateral relation of nonbeing, it thinks nonbeing as the structural determination of Blackness according to the Real—informed by the understanding that such thought cannot fulfill any of the integrationist dreams that make Black life possible while simultaneously being trapped in the position of the nonhuman.[60]

In her book *In the Wake*, Christina Sharpe recounts the difficulty of teaching a course that comparatively analyzed the Holocaust and North American slavery.[61] Most notable is her students' stubborn refusal to think of slavery as a system of violence—symptomatic of the pervasive discourse on history that imagines liberal democracy as a progressive march toward freedom. Enacting her own refusal of history as an attempt to insert distance between thought and slavery, she turns to the immanence of Blackness through Black scholarship that works to "stay in the hold of the ship."[62] Her interest in its afterlife does not stem from concerns about racial discrimination, colonial relations, or even white supremacy; rather, in elegantly restating the task as "living with immi/a/nent death," she considers anti-Blackness through the paradigm of a violence that is simultaneously imminent and already withdrawn.[63] So, on one hand, she explores contemporary anti-Blackness "with the obstructed passages of the Mediterranean, with carding, stop and frisk, the afterlives of *partus sequitur ventrem*, respiratory distress, detention centers, *Lagers*, and a multitude of other forms of surveillance."[64] On the other hand, she sits with the difficult notion that anti-Black violence is enduring because it is both atemporal and immanent.

The conclusion we should draw, as Sabine Broeck has also argued, is that Blackness throws into question the usefulness of history itself as an analytic, whereby New World slavery as an object of historiography has further rooted history in its "regime of European freedom of and as ownership, and of anti-Black abjection."[65] This argument is bolstered by Saidiya Hartman's contention about the unique relationship of Blackness to history, which requires a "history of failure" that is "written with and against the archive."[66] In some ways, the whole enterprise of modern philosophy and its subsequent political projects are based in the problems of genesis, structure, and transformation, from Marxism's historical tracing of the progression of forms to the Whiggist march toward emancipation. For both Marxists and Enlightenment liberals, the inability of the slave to shake its bondage is a sign of its inability to gain class consciousness and become a political subject of world-historical proportions. The reverse can be made true with the help of Laruelle, which is to say, that the task of Afro-pessimism is to abolish the role of historical development in thought and everything that such an abolition of history entails.

Uchromia: Nonrenewal

On March 3, 1991, the beating of Rodney King was recorded on a consumer video camera. The shaky footage shows police in a scene burned into so many minds that it need not be redescribed here. It showed the gruesome contradiction of Blackness: that the Black body as victim of brutality, even at its most vulnerable, is still made to appear as threatening, as if Blackness alone invites violence and death. The video was a media sensation and was considered essential evidence in legal proceedings, though a misplaced confidence in its depiction of shocking violence contributed to prosecutors' inability to attain a guilty verdict in the first trial. As true then as it is now, it was assumed that when photomedia "brings to light" police violence (through the assumed objectivity of the mechanical eye), accountability is all but assured. Yet the opposite is true:

when documented by police bodycams and citizen observers alike, the aesthetics of social death is put on loop, spreading images of violence that are simultaneously "shocking" and "objectively reasonable" in the eyes of the law.[67] Making such gratuitous violence visible does not inhibit the policing of Blackness but, in fact, enables it, a fact affirmed by social scientists who find that police who wear body cameras embolden officers often to commit more fatal shootings.[68] What then are we to make of the widespread impulse to spread summary executions across social media? Is there a Blackness-made-visible that does peddle in the libidinal economy of social death?

In their study of how the white ethics of social responsibility contributes to the violence of police profiling, Steve Martinot and Jared Sexton argue that "to focus on the spectacular event of police violence is to deploy (and thereby reaffirm) the logic of police profiling itself."[69] Consider, then, the beginning of *Scenes of Subjection*, where Saidiya Hartman notes her refusal to recount Fredrick Douglass's description of the beating of his Aunt Hester—"to call attention to the ease with which such scenes are usually reiterated, the casualness with which they are circulated, and the consequence of this routine display of the slave's ravaged body."[70] She goes on to explain that the empathic identification meant to be elicited by such scenes "cannot be extricated from the economy of chattel slavery" because they treat the slave's fungible, commodified body as an empty vessel "to don, occupy, or possess blackness or the black body as a sentimental resource and/or locus of enjoyment."[71] Similar aesthetic reiterations persist across a variety of mediums. A transitional medium between slave orations in antebellum speaking tours and today's digital media would be the lynching photographs popularly circulated as postcards during the early twentieth century. More recently, as intensified by ubiquitous access to the recording and dissemination technologies of smartphones, scenes of police summary executions of Black people have routinely saturated social media feeds and been played by television news networks. The ostensible aim is to combat such shootings by garnering empathy for the victims, yet it quickly feeds into the established practice of witnessing the spectacularization of suffering as a commodity to be traded.

What can be developed against the spectacular economy of reportage that justifies trafficking in Black death through journalistic logic? Can there then be a nonaesthetics of Blackness? Such a line of inquiry might begin with Laruelle's short work *The Concept of Non-Photography*. In it, Laruelle argues that too many conceive of photography through a realist mode that makes it into a "distanced, reified, deficient mode of perception."[72] This "realist illusion" treats it as a device of autofactualization.[73] It reduces photography to an act of faith—faith in perception, faith in the spontaneity of photographic knowledge, and faith in capturing various things "inscribed in the World" (the eye, the camera, techniques, objects, scene, or event).[74] One might add that even those who circulate images of Black death to challenge it hold faith in a similar automatic process, that depicting violence somehow brings about its end. Yet what remains automatic about photography is its fundamentally identificatory role, found in the mug shot, state identification cards, visas, and wanted posters.[75] There may be fleeting moments of resistance in this world, as Tina Campt has argued, with the fugitive study of the compelled poses of identification photos—yet it requires a shift in perspective, as in her suggestion for studying "black quiet."[76] Against the photographs' reiteration of the philosopher's belief in the world with every press of the button, Laruelle proposes a nonphotography.

Simone Browne has shown how the policing of Blackness is essential to understanding surveillance technologies. Through the term *black luminosity*, she investigates the policing techniques that use Blackness as the paradigmatic way to render bodies knowable through visibility, from eighteenth-century lantern laws to the more contemporary identification technologies of facial recognition.[77] Along similar lines, Anirban Gupta-Nigam has argued that Richard Dyer's history of cinematic lighting reveals the dominant aesthetic presupposition that whiteness is easily made transparent, while blackness always resists through a proximate opacity.[78] The conflict between these two perspectives is played out on a formal level whenever the color black is considered through addition or subtraction—for the light artist using additive color, blackness is the absence of color, while for a painter using subtractive color, blackness is the combination of all colors.[79] The consequence for Gupta-Nigam is that blackness is *trapped between an ontological state of withdrawal and a hypervisibility* produced through marking. These two poles establish an aesthetic economy of blackness that restates Frantz Fanon's comment that "I came into the world . . . at the crossroads between Nothingness and Infinity."[80] Ultimately, Gupta-Nigam warns that aesthetic approaches to blackness risk becoming a "regulative response to black priority" that thinks blackness through the analogy of visuality—light and darkness, visages and shadows—seeing it only in relief rather than thinking blackness in and of itself.[81] Instructive here is Patrice Douglass and Frank Wilderson's argument that any metaphysical speculation of blackness must remain grounded by a theory of violence.[82]

Against the backdrop of a spectacular violence simultaneously withdrawn and hypervisible, the aesthetics of blackness appears almost impossible. The pornotropic process of rendering the Black body as mere flesh seems to result in at least two polar outcomes: blackness gets objectified as an empty vessel or an indomitable vitality—something inert that gains life only when ventriloquized through possession or that is traded as fungible commodity—or as endowed with an unconquerable vibrancy euphemized as real, bold, deep, funky, raw, vivid, or loud.

In his 1988 "On the Black Universe: In the Human Foundations of Color," Laruelle radicalizes blackness by embracing it as the degree zero of light, color, humanity, the world, and even the universe itself.[83] Discussing it through Robert Fludd's black square from *Ultriusque Cosmi* (1671), Eugene Thacker distinguishes blackness from both theory of color and metaphor for ignorance. distinguishes between darkness that "always exists in some relation to light, however gradated, tenebrous, and shadowy," and blackness that is "anterior to both light and dark." A black universe, then, is not the cosmic study of a color but "the withdrawal of every relation between self and the world," resulting in a "breach" that "makes itself apparent as such."[84] Blackness here stands against the world, which remains all too human. Recognizing the risk of such abstract discussions lapsing into the sort of regulative response

Gupta-Nigam diagnoses, Alexander R. Galloway elaborates on the implications for blackness as a "crypto-ontology absolutely foreclosed to being":

> Channel that great saint of radical blackness, Toussaint Louverture, and return to the Haitian Constitution of 1804, which stated that all citizens will be called black regardless of color. Such blanket totality of black, such cataclysm of human color, renders color invalid and denies the endless dynamics of black-as-white or white-as-black. Black is no longer the limit case, no longer the case of the slave, the poor, the indentured or debt-ridden worker. Black is the foundation of a new uchromia, a new color utopia rooted in the generic black universe. "Our uchromia: to learn to think from the point of view of Black as what determines color in the last instance rather than what limits it."[85]

The passage reveals how closely non-philosophy converges with Black study. Both begin by dismissing the insufficiency of the small victories celebrated by the historical politics of contingency, and each identifies Blackness as crucial for bringing about the death of a world constituted through an incomplete concept of humanity ("a phenomenal blackness entirely fills the essence of man").[86]

Could the two approaches ultimately diverge? Laruelle's unique proposal is a uchromia, a noncolor, of blackness. Laruelle argues that epistemology has long relied on light-based metaphors to shuttle between confusion and knowledge, bondage and freedom, wrongness and rightness. It is right there in the name of the "Enlightenment." The connection is not incidental but metaphysical. Following a similar thread in Black thought, Wilderson has argued that "how we understand suffering and whether we locate its essence in economic exploitation or in anti-Blackness has a direct impact on how we imagine freedom; and on how we foment revolution."[87] He then criticizes Marxism for remaining invested in socialist emancipation narratives based in "equality, liberation, or redress" translated into aesthetic ideas.[88] At the structural level, "turning Absence into Presence is not the same as turning waged workers into free workers" because "the latter reorganizes the world; the former bring it to an end."[89] Why? Blackness inheres not in labor, gender, or land but as "the mark of slaveness."[90] The consequence is that Black positionality, "because it is without world(ly analogy), cannot articulate its demands in the grammar of the world"—or said otherwise, "it cannot emplot its demands in a narrative passage from present domination to the possibility of future liberation."[91] The result is that Afro-pessimism has no truck with the story of liberation so common to the Enlightenment and socialism: that the forces of human freedom are waiting to be unleashed through breaking of the remaining forms of bondage. So even if Galloway does not present a theory of suffering, perhaps he still identifies a point of convergence for the two projects in the aesthetics of light. Said another way, perhaps the abolition of the metaphysics of liberation can be at least partially an aesthetic one.

Unless carefully parsed, however, the conceptual foundations of such a Black universe could slip into either possessive liberalism or vitalism. If the French *Declaration of the Rights of Man and of the Citizen* is not so much invalidated but determined otherwise, it would only shift in who (ontologically) a citizen is. In its crudest form, such a universe would realize the neoliberal multicultural demand that white civil society be populated differently, with different faces in bigger places. More broadly, citizenship could still bear the same possessive individualism of liberal human rights, though Blackened by defining that citizenship by the condition of all individuals as *not* being proprietors of their own capacities—a sort of nonfreedom of incapacity.[92] Given the precision with which Black study theorizes the fungible Black body, the criticism of possessive liberalism needs less rehearsal—while, on the other hand, the vitalism interpretation may be far more likely; in it, blackness is taken to be the substrate of an *élan vital* that animates all color, life, or the cosmos. Such vitalism treats Blackness as an agency that persists even when held captive—something furtive, ineffable, richly capacious, that always escapes a structural condition.

Conflicting interpretations of the aesthetics of blackness are no more apparent than in recent writing about abstract art. Art historian Darby English proposes that conventions have formed a "black representation space" that prevents Black art from being truly seen, only considered from a viewpoint beyond the work of art itself.[93] He concretizes this concern through writing on David Hammon's 2002 installation *Concerto in Black and Blue* by art critics, who perform a vitalist overdetermining of the meaning of the piece while simultaneously failing to see any of the details that make it singular—"there is a sense . . . in which the entire history of Africans in North America can be told through reference to these two colors," he echoes from one, while another says that "bound up with the contemplation of the colors black and blue" is the "suggestion of the universality of African American Cultural Expression."[94]

In her writing about artist Adam Pendleton's abstract work *Black Sun* (2013–14), Adrienne Edwards is keenly aware of English's criticism.[95] "Blackness in abstraction," she writes, "shifts analysis away from the Black artist as subject and instead emphasizes blackness as material, method and mode, insisting on blackness as a multiplicity" so that "we can think of what it does in the world without conflating it . . . with a singular historical narrative or monolithic subjectivity."[96] Yet, at the same time, she describes the work through references to the cosmic ("a constellation," "Sun Ra"), the religious ("barbed" like a thorn crown), and the violent ("projectiles burst"), leading her to descriptions of vitalist plentitude, saying that Blackness, "in the fullest sense of the word, has a seemingly unlimited usefulness in the history of modern art" and is a "profound capaciousness."[97]

But what is the significance of treating Blackness as material, which is to say, a substance for theorization, speculation, or creativity? As Franco Barchiesi has argued, those who use new ontologies that look to "the self-constitution of collective political subjects in a continuous state of becoming" fail to grasp the fundamental constitution of Blackness through death, especially through its focus on capacity and relationality.[98] Putting a point on it, in a statement to the Humboldt Forum "Das Milieu Der Toten," Saidiya Hartman and Christina Sharpe said, "How do we attend to Black Death? A question we must return to again and again, since our suffering to the degree that it is recognized, is pornotropically exploited in the service of rehabilitating anti-black and colonial institutions. . . .

Don't use our death, our suffering, our lives and our work to regenerate your projects. Don't turn our flesh into gold again. We do not consent to this."[99]

Countless more abstract works appeal to Blackness through the cosmic register, but without ending on a redemptive note. Through concepts introduced by Fred Moten in "The Case of Blackness," Jared Sexton argues that abstraction tends to quarantine blackness from Blacks, separating color from people.[100] Here contrasting claims over an alleged racist inscription hidden under Kazimir Malevich's *Black Square* (1915) are ripe for debate—is there a secret anti-Black message cryptically sealed below the surface of the canonical piece of black abstraction?[101] Take, for example, Vincent Como's essay "The Black Singularity: To Know the Unknowable," namely, because it is an extensive treatment of the abstract blackness that fails to mention Black people. Does it perform the quarantining purification of blackness identified by Moten? Looking at starting points, Como's opening sentence curiously mirrors Afro-pessimism's fundamental concept of humanity being constituted out of the exclusion of blackness, as he states that black "is the constant through which humanity became manifest," while Sexton begins with the axiomatic premise that "it is evident that #BlackLivesMatter and the organizations that coalesce the Movement for Black Lives (M4BL) represent the most important and promising developments in the theory and practice of abolition."[102] Both essays also converge in their conclusions, with Como declaring that "Black is Everything. Everything is Nothing. Nothing is All," while Sexton states that "black is a color, noncolor, and all colors."[103] So rather than looking for a representation of people, he looks to how each formal arrangement of materials (monochromatic painting, black soap, and an assemblage of rice paper–mesh–acrylic–twine) forms a "conduit" between blackness-as-symbol and the concept of Black people, "rather than an obstacle to the concept," using the concrete, "in its infinite depth," to lead the viewer "toward rather than away from the universal and its infinite breadth."[104] It is those materials that enable Sexton to mention the events of the U.S. civil rights movement (the March on Washington for Jobs and Freedom), instruments of slave torture (the scarifying whip and chain), the conditions of sex work (the topic of P-Funk's "Cosmic Slop"), global slave cultures (including East Asia), flesh (skin and bones), and the history of confinement (steel and rope).[105]

In his closing to "All Black Everything," Sexton states that "Black is generous and generative, inclusive and encompassing."[106] But this statement need not swerve toward post-Spinozist versions of immanence that retain capacity as an animating force; one could turn to Laruelle, who defines blackness as determining all color yet not being a thing to possess or a force that is irrepressibly plentiful. Galloway's quotation rightfully selects determination in the last instance as a Laruellean alternative to blackness-as-limit and thus sidesteps the deconstructive *à venir* of French theory that poses things as necessary-impossible horizons for which to strive, even if they never arrive (Derrida's democracy to come, Agamben's coming community). The prefix *non-* uses metaphysics as a raw material to discover the logics of real immanence therein. The generic blackness of uchromia is not a potent force, a generative substance, or a horizon but an opacity—the pointing out of the insufficiency of the whole philosophical endeavor and the failure of its categories of thought ("history," "the human," "liberation"). In this framework, blackness escapes the dialectical antagonism of the poisoned gift—a "fundamental dependency" that "paradoxically, initiates and sustains our agency"—because it does not seek refuge in whiteness (representation) or lightness (reason).[107] This is because the point of blackness is not to reproduce the world but to abolish it. Or to echo Sexton's own words, "slavery is the threshold of the political world, abolition the interminable radicalization of every radical movement."[108]

Conclusion

One of Afro-pessimism's most important contributions is its only concrete prescription: simply to sit with the difficulty of Blackness. This may not sit easy for those steeped in poststructuralist approaches to the cultural politics of difference. The initial political import of poststructuralism came from the novel suggestion that it provided the intellectual tools for fighting a sort of guerrilla war based on formal asymmetry, as marginality, difference, contingency, excess, and other aspects of an "inferior" position were recast not as weaknesses but as strengths. Yet with enough time, poststructuralist theories of the in-between, molecularity, resistance, and antagonism (to name a few) have been chewed up by reformists and spit out as "finding the answer somewhere in the middle," "unexpected collaborations," "using the system against itself," and "deliberative democracy." If one were to look deeply enough, one might conclude that the structure of feeling of poststructuralism planted a particular fetish deep in scholars' psyches, resulting in the incessant yearning for certain symbols of resistance to be possessed, praised, and circulated. It is here that Afro-pessimism and non-philosophy coincide, simultaneously turning away from solutions and instead declaring the insufficiency of history, the human, the world—everything.

Insufficiency marks a refusal of poststructuralism's energetics by withdrawing from theories of subjective capacity, the tactical deployment of history as contingent, and aesthetic renewal. The genericness of the paradigm treats historical contingency with indifference. The zero degree of subjectivity knows the empty betrayal of enhanced capacities. The uchromia of the Black universe refuses the poisoned gift of aesthetic renewal. Concretely, it abandons the narrow recognition of the ballot box, it chooses not to establish worth on a ledger, and it does not try to prove the depth of its suffering in the frames of citizen recordings. Contrary to active-ist critics, such pessimism should not be confused for inaction, as these moves abolish the philosophical distinction between the abstract and the concrete (and the very distinction between thought and action). This is to say, it embodies the "destructive character" who opens with the ground-clearing move of an unflinching criticism of the "long game" of accumulating liberal democratic rights as if it would eventually conclude in human liberation, only to see past the abstractions keeping real work from being done.[109] The usual political project of coalitions will not do here, for they ask for Blackness to offer as a token in the form of historical, experiential, or aesthetic forms to be shared by the coalition.[110] It means taking axioms like Black Lives Matter as real, asking for them to be recognized not by the putative powers that be but by bringing to an end the authority of those who violently police the boundary of the human. As such, it takes up the mantle of abolitionism kept alive by Black militants and revolutionaries who have long fought in the streets, prisons, and everywhere else where slavery is found. And this time, instead of a new manumission, the task calls for nothing short of the generalized deracination of all of humanity brought by abolishing history, killing this world, and draining it of color.

Notes

1. Frank B. Wilderson III, *Red, White, and Black: Cinema and the Structure of U.S. Antagonisms* (Durham, N.C.: Duke University Press, 2010), ix.
2. Nahum Dimitri Chandler, *X—The Problem of the Negro as a Problem for Thought* (New York: Fordham University Press, 2014), 11–19.
3. Frank B. Wilderson III, "I Am Frank Wilderson AMA," Reddit, November 1, 2016, https://www.reddit.com/r/Debate/comments/5al9pl/i_am_frank_wilderson_ama/.
4. Selamawit Terrefe and Christina Sharpe, "What Exceeds the Hold? An Interview with Christina Sharpe," *Rhizomes*, no. 29 (2016): 78.
5. Anthony Paul Smith, *Laruelle: A Stranger to Thought* (Cambridge: Polity, 2016), 94–97, 112–18.
6. There are various inconsistencies about the remarks in the historical record, but it appears that the most comprehensive account is cited by Natalie Robertson, "Stolen Away," in *Freedom in My Heart: Voices from the United States National Slavery Museum*, ed. Cynthia Jacobs Carter (Washington, D.C.: U.S. National Slavery Museum, in association with National Geographic, 2008), 72. An official transcript of the proceedings confirms the general contour of the remarks; see Gregson v. Gilbert, 3 Sylvester Douglas 232 (1783). The comments are further confirmed through the memoirs of a famous abolitionist, but through comment by the case's chief judge Lord Mansfield; see Prince Hoare, *Memoirs of Granville Sharp, Esq* (London: Henry Colburn, 1820), 241.
7. An explicit example of how Kant's transcendental method forms an aporia that motivates additional thought would be Foucault's writing on his anthropology. Michel Foucault, "Introduction to Kant's Anthropology from a Pragmatic Point of View," trans. Arianna Bove, Generation Online, 2002, http://www.generation-online.org/p/fpfoucault1.htm, though this could be taken as a starting point for nearly all of poststructuralism as well as a significant portion of modern philosophy.

8. Frank B. Wilderson III, "Biko and the Problematic of Presence," in *Biko Lives!*, ed. Andile Mngxitama, Amanda Alexander, and Nigel C. Gibson (New York: Palgrave Macmillan, 2008), 95.
9. François Laruelle, *Introduction to Non-Marxism*, trans. Anthony Paul Smith (Minneapolis: Univocal, 2014), 108.
10. Orlando Patterson, *Slavery and Social Death* (Cambridge, Mass,: Harvard University Press, 1982).
11. See, e.g., Jared Sexton, "'The Curtain of the Sky': An Introduction," *Critical Sociology* 36, no. 1 (2010): 11–24; an essential interlocutor here is David Marriott.
12. Jean-Paul Sartre, *Anti-Semite and Jew*, trans. George Joseph Becker (New York: Schocken Books, 1948), 8, 38.
13. Jared Sexton, "Afro-Pessimism: The Unclear Word," *Rhizomes*, no. 29 (2016).
14. Wilderson, "Biko and the Problematic of Presence," 97.
15. Shannon Walsh and Frank B. Wilderson III, "Afro-Pessimism and Friendship in South Africa," in *Ties That Bind: Race and the Politics of Friendship*, ed. Shannon Walsh and Jon Soske (Johannesburg: Wits University Press, 2017), 78–79.
16. Sharon Patricia Holland, *Raising the Dead: Readings of Death and (Black) Subjectivity* (Durham, N.C.: Duke University Press, 2000), 15.
17. At least two of Hortense Spillers's essays in *Black, White, and in Color: Essays on American Literature and Culture* (Chicago: University of Chicago Press, 2003) are crucial here: "Mama's Baby, Papa's Maybe: An American Grammar Book" and "Interstices: A Small Drama of Words." In the latter, see page 155.
18. Jean-Luc Nancy, *Being Singular Plural* (Stanford, Calif.: Stanford University Press, 2000), 47.
19. Nancy, 47.
20. Philippe Lacoue-Labarthe and Jean-Luc Nancy, *Retreating the Political*, ed. Simon Sparks (London: Routledge, 1997), 108.
21. François Laruelle, *The Concept of Non-Photography*, trans. Robin Mackay (Falmouth, U.K.: Sequence Press, 2011), 123.
22. Alexander R. Galloway, *Laruelle: Against the Digital* (Minneapolis: University of Minnesota Press, 2014), 16.
23. Sabine Broeck, "'It Is Always Now' (Beloved): Notes on the Urgency of Enslavism Theory, and Studies," *Zeitschrift für Anglistik und Amerikanistik* 65, no. 2 (2017): 139.
24. François Laruelle, *General Theory of Victims*, trans. Alex Dubilet and Jessie Hock (Cambridge: Polity, 2015), 112–13.

25. Galloway, *Laruelle: Against the Digital*, 182.
26. Galloway, 182.
27. Echoing the "degree-zero of subjectivity" mentioned earlier, Laruelle holds that "the victim" is at the core of his ethical system—a victim who has been victimized beyond the point of death, made so absent that even the fact that the victim had once existed is under erasure.
28. From the book version of "Mama's Baby, Papa's Maybe," in Spillers, *Black, White, and in Color*, 205–9.
29. Giorgio Agamben, *The Use of Bodies*, trans. Adam Kotsko (Stanford, Calif.: Stanford University Press, 2016), 268.
30. Jared Sexton, "People-of-Color-Blindness: Notes on the Afterlife of Slavery," *Social Text* 28, no. 2 (2010): 31–56; Alexander G. Weheliye, *Habeas Viscus: Racializing Assemblages, Biopolitics, and Black Feminist Theories of the Human* (Durham, N.C.: Duke University Press, 2014).
31. Subsequent theorization can be found in works like Stefan Nowotny, "The Double Meaning of Destitution," trans. Aileen Derieg, European Institute for Progressive Cultural Policies, May 2007, http://eipcp.net/transversal/0507/nowotny/en.html.
32. The Invisible Committee, *Now*, trans. Robert Hurley (Los Angeles: Semiotext(e), 2017).
33. François Laurelle, "The Generic as Predicate and Constant: Non-Philosophy and Materialism," in *The Speculative Turn: Continental Materialism and Realism*, ed. Levi Bryant, Nick Srnicek, and Graham Harman, trans. Taylor Adkins, 237–60 (Melbourne: re.press, 2011).
34. Smith, *Laruelle*, 104–10.
35. Essential source material is Emmanuel Chukwudi Eze, *Race and the Enlightenment: A Reader* (Malden, Mass.; Blackwell, 1997), but there are substantial debates on Fanon and Hegel's use of the master–slave dialectic, especially in Gordon, Buck-Morss, Sexton, and Marriott. See also the work of Achille Mbembe, such as "Faces of Freedom: Jewish and Black Experiences," *Interventions* 7, no. 3 (2004): 293–98, in which the author covers the rapport between freedom and capacity in French responses to Hegel's "bondsman."
36. Spillers, *Black, White, and in Color*, 206.
37. Jared Sexton, "Unbearable Blackness," keynote lecture, October 25, 2012, https://vimeo.com/52199779.
38. Jared Sexton, "The Vel of Slavery: Tracking the Figure of Unsovereign," *Critical Sociology* 42, no. 4–5 (2014): 11.

39. Frantz Fanon, *Black Skin, White Masks*, trans. Richard Philcox (New York: Grove, 2008), 76.
40. Wilderson, "Biko and the Problematic of Presence"; IMIXWHATILIKE, "'We Are Trying to Destroy the World' Anti-Blackness & Police Violence After Ferguson: An Interview with Frank B. Wilderson, III," in *Shifting Corporealities in Contemporary Performance*, ed. Marina Gržinić and Aneta Stojnić (Cham, Switzerland: Palgrave Macmillan, 2018), 45–59; *Red, White, and Black: Cinema and the Structure of U.S. Antagonisms*; "The Vengeance of Vertigo: Aphasia and Abjection in the Political Trials of Black Insurgents," in *On Marronage: Ethical Confrontations with Antiblackness*, ed. P. Khalil Saucier and Tryon P. Woods (Trenton: Africa World Press, 2016); Jared Sexton, "'The Curtain of the Sky': An Introduction," *Critical Sociology* 36, no. 1 (2010):11–24; Sexton, "The Social Life of Social Death: On Afro-pessimism and Black Optimism," in *Time, Temporality and Violence in International Relations*, ed. Anna M. Agathangelou and Kyle D. Killian (London: Routledge, 2016); Jared Sexton, "Unbearable Blackness." *Cultural Critique* 90 (2015): 159–78; Jason R. Ambroise and Sabine Broeck, *Black Knowledges/ Black Struggles: Essays in Critical Epistemology* (Liverpool: Liverpool University Press, 2015); Warren, Calvin L., "Black Nihilism and the Politics of Hope," *New Centennial Review* 15, no. 1 (2015): 215–48; Warren, "Onticide: Afro-pessimism, ~~Gay~~ Nigger #1, and Surplus Violence," *GLQ: A Journal of Lesbian and Gay Studies* 23, no. 3 (2017): 391–418, https://www.muse.jhu.edu/article/659880; Warren, *Ontological Terror: Blackness, Nihilism, and Emancipation* (Durham, N.C.: Duke University Press, 2018); Sara-Maria Sorentino, "The Sociogeny of Social Death: Blackness, Modernity, and Its Metaphors in Orlando Patterson," *Rhizomes* 29 (2016), http://www.rhizomes.net/issue29/sorentino.html; M. Shadee Malaklou, "On the Chronopolitics of Black Social Life; or, How Mister Winfield 'Sends Go'"; and Eva Hayward and Che Gossett, "Impossibility of *That*."
41. Daniel Colucciello Barber, "World-Making and Grammatical Impasse," *Qui Parle: Critical Humanities and Social Sciences* 25, no. 1–2 (2016): 179–206.
42. Smith, *Laruelle*, 104.
43. Smith.
44. Terrell Jermaine Starr, "These Black People Are Making a Political Statement by Not Voting in the 2016 Election," *Splinter*, May 12,

2016, https://splinternews.com/these-black-people-are-making-a-political-statement-by-1793856760.

45. Hari Ziyad, "Op-Ed: Black People Who Do Note Vote Are Not Stupid, and Many Vote Pushers Are Anti-Black," *Afropunk*, April 27, 2017, https://afropunk.com/2017/04/op-ed-black-people-who-dont-vote-are-not-stupid-and-many-vote-pushers-are-anti-black/.
46. Frank B. Wilderson III, "Why I Don't Vote," October 17, 2016, 6, https://www.academia.edu/29401599/Why_I_Don_t_Vote.doc.
47. Calvin L. Warren, "Black Nihilism and the Politics of Hope," *New Centennial Review* 15, no. 1 (2015): 215–48.
48. Fanon, *Black Skin, White Masks*, 12.
49. Fanon.
50. Jared Sexton, "Ante-Anti-Blackness," *Lateral: Journal of the Cultural Studies Association*, no. 1 (2012).
51. François Laruelle, *The Transcendental Method*, ed. Robin Mackay, trans. Christopher Eby (Falmouth, U.K.: Urbanomic, 2012), 143.
52. Frank B. Wilderson III, "The Black Liberation Army and the Paradox of Political Engagement," in *Postcoloniality, Decoloniality, Black Critique: Joints and Fissures*, ed. Sabine Broeck and Carsten Junker (Frankfurt: Campus, 2014), 17.
53. Jaye Austin Williams and Frank B. Wilderson III, "Staging (within) Violence: A Conversation with Frank Wilderson and Jaye Austin Williams," *Rhizomes*, no. 29 (2016).
54. See also Sexton, "People-of-Color-Blindness."
55. Crucial here is Hortense Spillers's essay on psychoanalysis and race at the end of *Black, White, and in Color*, 394.
56. Kevin Quashie, *The Sovereignty of Quiet* (New Brunswick, N.J.: Rutgers University Press, 2012), 120.
57. Greg Thomas and Sylvia Wynter, "Proud Flesh Inter/Views: Sylvia Wynter," *ProudFlesh: New Afrikan Journal of Culture, Politics, and Consciousness*, no. 4 (2006); Wynter, "Unsettling the Coloniality of Being/Power/Truth/Freedom: Towards the Human, after Man, Its Overrepresentation—an Argument," *New Centennial Review* 3, no. 3 (2003): 257–337.
58. François Laruelle, "Identity and Event," trans. Ray Brassier, *Pli* 9 (2000): 174–89; Ray Brassier, "Solar Catastrophe: Lyotard, Freud, and the Death-Drive," *Philosophy Today* 47, no. 4 (2003): 421–30.
59. Kieran Aarons, "No Selves to Abolish: Afro-Pessimism, Anti-Politics, and the End of the World," *Hostis* 2 (2016): 103–27.
60. Saidiya V. Hartman and Frank B. Wilderson III, "The Position of

the Unthought," *Qui Parle: Critical Humanities and Social Sciences* 13, no. 2 (2003): 185.

61. Christina Sharpe, *In The Wake: On Blackness and Being* (Durham, N.C.: Duke University Press, 2016), 11–13.

62. Sharpe, 13–15.

63. Sharpe, 132, 5.

64. Sharpe, 132.

65. Sabine Broeck, "Legacies of Enslavism and White Abjectorship," in *Postcoloniality, Decoloniality, Black Critique: Joints and Fissures*, ed. Sabine Broeck and Carsten Junker (Frankfurt: Campus, 2014), 5–9, 13.

66. Saidiya V. Hartman, "Venus in Two Acts," *Small Axe* 12, no. 2 (2008): 12.

67. Ben Brucato, "Policing Made Visible: Mobile Technologies and the Importance of Point of View," *Surveillance and Society* 13, no. 3/4 (2015): 466–68.

68. Min-Seok Pang and Paul A. Pavlou, "Armed with Technology: The Impact on Fatal Shootings by the Police," Fox School of Business Research Paper 16-020 (2016).

69. Steve Martinot and Jared Sexton, "The Avant-Garde of White Supremacy," *Social Identities* 9, no. 2 (2003): 173.

70. Saidiya V. Hartman, *Scenes of Subjection: Terror, Slavery, and Self-Making in Nineteenth-Century America* (Oxford: Oxford University Press, 1997), 3.

71. Hartman, 21.

72. Laruelle, *Concept of Non-Photography*, 8.

73. Laruelle.

74. Laruelle.

75. Laruelle, 27.

76. Tina Campt, *Listening to Images* (Durham, N.C.: Duke University Press, 2017).

77. Simone Browne, *Dark Matters On the Surveillance of Blackness* (Durham, N.C.: Duke University Press, 2015), 67–68.

78. Anirban Gupta-Nigam, "Black Infrastructure: Media and the Trap of Visibility," *Media Fields Journal*, no. 11 (2016): 1–11. John Gillespie has persuasively argued that it is a hyperreal overrepresentation; see Gillespie, "On the Prospect of Weaponized Death," *Propter Nos* 2, no. 1 (2017): 5–11.

79. Johannes Itten, *The Elements of Color*, trans. Ernst Van Hagen (New York: John Wiley, 1970), 17.

80. Fanon, *Black Skin, White Masks*, 89, 119.

81. Gupta-Nigam, "Black Infrastructure," 8.
82. Patrice Douglass and Frank B. Wilderson III, "The Violence of Presence: Metaphysics in a Blackened World," *The Black Scholar* 43, no. 4 (2013): 117–23.
83. Eugene Thacker, *Starry Speculative Corpse: Horror of Philosophy* (Winchester, U.K.: Zero Books, 2015), 60, 52.
84. Thacker, 51.
85. Galloway, *Laruelle: Against the Digital*, 145.
86. François Laurelle, "On the Black Universe: In the Human Foundations of Color," in *Dark Nights of the Universe*, ed. Eugene Thacker et al. (Miami: NAME, 2013), 105.
87. Wilderson, "Biko and the Problematic of Presence," 97.
88. Wilderson, "The Black Liberation Army and the Paradox of Political Engagement," 178.
89. Wilderson, "Biko and the Problematic of Presence," 100.
90. Daniel Colucciello Barber, "World-Making and Grammatical Impasse," *Qui Parle: Critical Humanities and Social Sciences* 25, no. 1–2 (2016): 188.
91. Barber, 191.
92. Crawford Brough Macpherson, *The Political Theory of Possessive Individualism: Hobbes to Locke* (Oxford: Clarendon Press, 1962), 3.
93. Darby English, *How to See a Work of Art in Total Darkness* (Cambridge, Mass.: MIT Press, 2007), 3, 6.
94. English, 4.
95. Adrienne Edwards, "Blackness in Abstraction," *Art in America* (blog), January 5, 2015, https://web.archive.org/web/20161107032917/http://www.artinamericamagazine.com/news-features/magazine/blackness-in-abstraction/.
96. Edwards.
97. Edwards.
98. Franco Barchiesi, "Precarity as Capture: A Conceptual Reconstruction and Critique of the Worker-Slave Analogy," *Ponencia Presentada en el Coloquio Internacional* 5 (2012).
99. Saidiya V. Hartman and Christina Sharpe, "Statement from Saidiya Hartman and Christina Sharpe at the Humboldt Forum," 2017, https://processedlives.tumblr.com/post/168319118010/last-night-saidiya-hartman-began-with-a-question.
100. Jared Sexton, "All Black Everything," *E-Flux*, no. 79 (February 2017): 5.
101. Hot takes of the announcement by researchers at Russia's State Tretyakov Gallery, such as Dunne, "Art Historians Find Racist

Joke Hidden under Malevich's 'Black Square,'" and art historians looking to shore up Malevich's legacy, as in Aleksandra Shatskikh, "Inscribed Vandalism: The Black Square at One Hundred," *E-Flux*, no. 85 (October 2017): 1–10.

102. Vincent Como, "The Black Singularity: To Know the Unknowable," *Drain* (blog), 2015, http://drainmag.com/the-black-singularity/; Sexton, "All Black Everything," 1.
103. Como, "Black Singularity"; Sexton, "All Black Everything," 10.
104. Sexton, "All Black Everything," 8. A Laruellean approach would characterize the black as universal and *finite*.
105. Sexton, 8–10.
106. Sexton, 10.
107. Judith Butler, quoted in Sexton, 10.
108. Sexton, "Vel of Slavery," 11.
109. Walter Benjamin, "The Destructive Character," in *Reflections: Essays, Aphorisms, Autobiographic Writings*, trans. Edmund Jephcott (New York: Harcourt Brace Jovanovich, 1978), 301–3.
110. Frank B. Wilderson III, "The Prison Slave as Hegemony's (Silent) Scandal," *Social Justice* 30, no. 2 (2003): 18–27.

Contributors

Joshua Clover is professor of English and comparative literature at the University of California, Davis and an affiliated professor of literature and modern culture at the University of Copenhagen.

Andrew Culp teaches media history and theory in the aesthetics and politics program and the School of Critical Studies at the California Institute of the Arts. His *Dark Deleuze* (Minnesota, 2016) has been translated into several languages, and he is also author of *A Guerrilla Guide to Refusal* (Minnesota, 2022).

Kennan Ferguson teaches political theory at the University of Wisconsin–Milwaukee (UWM). He is coeditor of the journal *Theory and Event* and author of several books, including *Cookbook Politics* and *All in the Family: On Community and Incommensurability*. From 2015 to 2017, he directed the Center for 21st Century Studies at UWM.

Katerina Kolozova is professor of philosophy and political science. Her books include *Capitalism's Holocaust of Animals: A Non-Marxist Critique of Capital, Philosophy, and Patriarchy*, and *Cut of the Real: Subjectivity in Poststructuralist Philosophy*. She has been a member of the International Organization of Non-Philosophy, based in Paris, France, since its inception.

François Laruelle is associate professor of philosophy, doctor of state, and professor emeritus of general and contemporary philosophy at the University of Paris Ouest Nanterre. He is author of *Philosophy and Non-Philosophy* and *Dictionary of Non-Philosophy*, both available from the University of Minnesota Press.

Theodore Martin is associate professor of English at the University of California, Irvine and author of *Contemporary Drift: Genre, Historicism, and the Problem of the Present*.

Anthony Paul Smith is associate professor in La Salle University's Department of Religion and Theology. He is translator of a number of works by François Laruelle and author of *Laruelle: A Stranger Thought*.

Frank B. Wilderson III is professor and chair of African American studies and a core faculty member of the culture and theory PhD program at the University of California, Irvine. He is author of *Afropessimism*; *Incognegro: A Memoir of Exile and Apartheid*; and *Red, White, and Black: Cinema and the Structure of U.S. Antagonisms*.

Index